THE STORY OF

WALDORF EDUCATION

IN THE UNITED STATES

THE STORY OF
WALDORF EDUCATION
IN THE UNITED STATES

Past, Present, and Future

Stephen Keith Sagarin

STEINERBOOKS
2011

SteinerBooks
610 Main Street, Great Barrington, MA 01230
www.steinerbooks.org

Library of Congress Cataloging-in-Publication Data

Sagarin, Stephen Keith.
 The story of Waldorf education in the United States : past, present, and
future / Stephen Keith Sagarin.
     p. cm.
Includes bibliographical references.
ISBN 978-0-88010-656-6
1. Waldorf method of education — United States — History. I. Title.
LB1029.W34S27 2011
371.39'10973—dc23

                          2011034720

Contents

To my family,
my students,
my colleagues,
and my teachers.

Introduction

AFTER ATTENDING THREE DIFFERENT PUBLIC SCHOOLS through eighth grade, I attended high school at the Waldorf School of Garden City from 1977 to 1980. I had good teachers at all the schools I attended, and some not-so-good ones, too. But the Waldorf School felt, as I've said many times since, "like coming home."

Partly, it was that the school treated education as an extension of life and home. In our pre-Waldorf days, for instance, my mother never told us what she was doing, but when we got home from public school, she would sit my brothers and me down and teach us to knit. Or paint or draw or model in clay. She read to us in the evenings, and she drew pictures for us. She was a pianist, and we all played instruments. We hiked through the woods, we watched birds and deer. We split and stacked wood, fed the chickens, turned soil in the garden. I don't believe the word even existed in the late 1960s and 1970s, but she was supplementing our public school education with what we might now call Waldorf homeschooling. These activities—I remember particularly those in the arts and those in nature—somehow blended seamlessly into life, including academic and athletic activities, once we enrolled at the suburban Waldorf School. This worked, not because of external similarities among the different things we did, but because of the sense of meaning and purpose shared by the adults.

Although my teachers at the Waldorf School varied widely in talent (at least from my callow point of view), and although I felt great affinity for some and far less for others, they all shared a unity of purpose that, although they didn't speak about it to their students, was evident in how they treated us. In my other schools, classrooms and teachers were too frequently disconnected from one another. In English, there was no acknowledgement of science or math, or of the science teacher, Mr. Gearing, or the math teacher, Mrs. Miller. It was as if each teacher and each subject was vacuum-sealed and shelved. At the Waldorf School, things were generally otherwise. The teachers knew, acknowledged, and valued each other's work. They knew what each student was doing in each class, more or less, and they also cared about what was happening in our lives outside of school. Further, they shared a belief that the world was meaningful and that, through teaching, they could help us to find it meaningful as well. What could be better for adolescents?

For a graduation speech, the faculty chair (a position as close to headmistress as a Waldorf school gets) wanted me to speak about the differences between my years at Waldorf and my years in public school. But, at 18, I had not digested these differences in the slightest; I didn't want to seem to acknowledge them, or to care. I was too close to them. I couldn't honestly say that I would have been that much different if I had stayed in public school. Now, looking back more than three decades, I can say I would not be who I am—and you would not now be reading this book—had I not attended the Waldorf School.

As it was, I could not acknowledge my misgivings about contrasting my years at Waldorf and my years in public school, so I wrote a sham speech for the faculty chair, and wrote the real one at home, on my own. Only my mother and one classmate knew what I was up to.

Graduation day arrived. I stood at the podium in my new suit and I delivered the speech I wanted to give. There was nothing revolutionary or offensive in it. It just wasn't the one the faculty chair expected. I avoided eye contact with her and plunged ahead. Sorry, Mrs. Scherer. If I had it to do over again, I would tell you that the topic you chose for me was simply too difficult; that it would require a few decades of teaching, experience, research, and thinking to acknowledge and to address. This book, although it does not compare Waldorf education with conventional or public school education, is partly a result of my early awakening to the way things were different in the Waldorf School I attended.

Backing up for a moment, I will mention that, during my junior year of high school, the Waldorf School went through a terrible time, losing perhaps half the teachers and many students over a disagreement that I'll detail later in the book. These teachers who had seemed to share such a unity of purpose were now virtually at war with one another. How could this be? This tension between the shared ideals and the difficult realities that faced these men and women whom I so admired also served to arouse questions in me that this book aims to address.

Finally, after I graduated from college, to make a longer story shorter, I found myself teaching at the same Waldorf School I had attended. As I grew into my job, I began to realize that Waldorf schools were not static, and that they were not produced from a cookie-cutter. As I started to study Rudolf Steiner's writings and lectures on education, I found real differences between what I read and what my colleagues and I were doing. I also noticed real differences between the way things were done in Garden City and the way I found they were done elsewhere; for example, at the nearby Rudolf Steiner School in New York City. Acknowledging these differences and looking into their histories and, in particular, the thinking behind them, has contributed, too, to the impulse to write this book.

For whom, then, is this book written?

If you know nothing at all about Waldorf schools and Waldorf education, this book will, I hope, introduce them to you in a sympathetic but clear-eyed way. You will learn how Waldorf and Steiner schools (there is no difference between these labels) have grown in the United States, and what the major distinctions among them are and have been. I will give you a framework for understanding this history in a way that clarifies the origins of many of the differences among Waldorf schools—and many of the stereotypes about them—and that leaves room for other interpretations.

You will also learn how others have defined or described what we call "Waldorf education"—a phrase that Rudolf Steiner, the founder of the first Waldorf School, rarely used. I believe there are serious problems with many previous attempts to define Waldorf education, however, and I offer a view that I believe expands beyond these.

If you know about Waldorf education (let's say you're a young teacher, or a parent of students at a Waldorf school, or a graduate of a Waldorf school) but are primarily familiar with one school, this book, I hope, will broaden your horizons and deepen your understanding of what you or your children are up to.

If you are an experienced Waldorf school teacher, someone who has worked at or visited other schools, who has experience across several years, then my hope is that this book will deepen your appreciation for the history of which you are a part, and broaden your understanding of it. I also aim to offer a view of Waldorf education that separates wheat from chaff, or myths from essentials. In doing so, even if readers disagree with my findings, I hope to provide a platform and method for working in a similar way toward a better understanding of what those of us in Waldorf schools are about.

This book is in no way, however, an attempt to teach anyone what it means to be a Waldorf school teacher, or how to teach according to Steiner's methods. Many such books exist already, and the work required (whether in a formal teacher educa-tion program, in on-the-job training, or simply through reading Steiner's three hundred-some lectures on education, not to men-tion the veritable library of books on teaching and learning that Waldorf schools have spawned) is completely outside the scope or aim of this book.

This book is an attempt to take a hard look at Waldorf education and Waldorf schools in the United States and to understand their history, and what we might colloquially call their "philosophy" (although a better word would be "method") on their own terms. By a "hard look" I mean one that takes Steiner's work seriously, but not one that swallows it whole, unexamined and indigestible. This book attempts to understand the history and method of Waldorf schools according to the work of their founders, and also in the context of the promises and compromises that these schools and teachers have made, knowingly and unknowingly, across the years since the first Waldorf School was founded in 1919.

The first portion of this book is a history of Waldorf schools in the United States from the first school in New York City, founded in 1928, through schools founded at the turn of the twenty-first century. Waldorf schools are schools that use the educational methods, examined in the first part of this book, propounded by Rudolf Steiner, Austrian philosopher, seer, and educator (1861–1925); they are most often named after the first such school, the Independent Waldorf School, in Stuttgart, Germany. This school was independent of the German state educational system, and was named for the corporation that sponsored it: the Waldorf-Astoria cigarette factory (Staley 1998).

Steiner's method has been updated to consider such topics as educational technology and learning differences. Cursory examination reveals a tension here between strict adherence to Steiner's words and the demands of particular situations. I characterize this tension as the tension between promise and compromise. What course can schools chart that remains true to Steiner's conception of education but doesn't devolve into dogma or dissolve into convention? This question is necessarily at the heart of any consideration of the history of Waldorf schools. Ida Oberman (1999), for example, characterizes a similar tension as one between "form" and "flexibility."

Beyond Oberman's work, however, there is virtually nothing written that concerns the general history of Waldorf schools or

Steiner's method in the United States. I have considered Oberman's work in a few places later, but one aspect deserves initial mention. Oberman examines the history of Waldorf schools
starting from the original school in Stuttgart, Germany, founded
in 1919, through the Milwaukee Urban Waldorf School, founded
in 1991. In particular, she traces the history of the transplantation
of Waldorf schools from Germany to the United States. That is
something I will not do.

In the last portion of her work, which deals with schools in the
United States, Oberman defines three generations and suggests
that a fourth is blossoming. One of my fundamental insights, the
realization of which drove me to write this book, concerns this
division of history into generations. I was a student at the Waldorf
School of Garden City in the 1970s, and I taught there in the
1980s and 1990s. Attending conferences at other Waldorf schools,
it became clear to me that the cultures of Waldorf schools, while
fundamentally similar, vary greatly depending on the periods in
which the schools were founded.

Specifically, I will divide the history of Waldorf schools in the
United States into generations that I call (with a nod to Henry
James) "The Europeans," from the founding of the first school,
the Rudolf Steiner School in New York City in 1928, roughly
through World War II; "The Americans," from World War II
through the mid-1960s; "The Alternatives," from the mid-1960s
through the early 1990s; and "The Social Missionaries," from the
1990s to the present.

Oberman sees the first three of these generations aiming at
"purity," "accommodation," and "evolution." These are concepts
that characterize an inward-facing quality of the schools, what
they might say to each other about their interpretations of Steiner's work. By contrast, I have chosen to characterize these generations according to external influences, seeing each as a product
of its time and its place in the development of Waldorf schooling in the United States. The first generation shows a European
influence; the second, an American influence; and the third, a

countercultural or "alternative" influence. The fourth generation demonstrates an attempt to recover what might be called
Steiner's "social mission" for Waldorf education. I end this section
with a brief look at the possible futures of Waldorf education,
given what we know of the growth and development of Waldorf
schools in the United States and what we know of its present
configurations, trends, and challenges.

Part Two of the book concerns definitions and characteriza-
tions of what has come to be called Waldorf education. I examine
others' strategies for defining or describing Waldorf education;
examine some common myths or stereotypes of Waldorf education; and then attempt to point to what we might call the essentials of Waldorf education.

What Is a Waldorf School?

If, as I claim toward the end of this book, there is actually
no such thing as "Waldorf education," then what is a Waldorf
or Steiner school? I believe a simple definition will suffice for
the moment. Any school that claims that its educational method
originates with Rudolf Steiner can be held (in this book) to be
a Waldorf school. The term "Waldorf" is used because the first
school, in Stuttgart, Germany, was called the "Independent Waldorf School." The term "Waldorf" denoted that the school was
a subsidiary of the Waldorf-Astoria cigarette factory, initially for
the children of whose workers the school was founded. The word
"independent" was used because the school was self-administered
rather than administered by the state government. (See, for example, Betty Staley's excellent introduction to Steiner's conferences
with the teachers in the first school, 1998.)

The Association of Waldorf Schools of North America
(AWSNA) has a service mark for the names "Waldorf" and
"Rudolf Steiner" in the United States as they apply to education,
and uses a narrower definition. According to AWSNA (2003),
only an independent school can be a Waldorf school; attempts to

use Steiner's methods in a public school must be called "Waldorf-inspired" or "Waldorf methods schools." Many in Waldorf schools subscribe to this idea, but many others subscribe to the different idea that any school courageous enough to attempt to put Steiner's ideas about education into practice must necessarily compromise part of the mission of the schooling in order to pursue the promise these methods contain. Such a school should be allowed, if it chooses, to call itself a Waldorf school. All of the founding schools of AWSNA enjoyed this freedom. More on this later.

Steiner School Archive

The Rudolf Steiner School in New York kindly provided access to its archive of minutes from faculty and board of directors meetings from 1930 to 1950. With a few exceptions, noted in the text, the entire chapter called "The Europeans" relies on this archive. Unfortunately, I did not have similar access to minutes from later schools, and so subsequent chapters required different sources.

Self-Published Literature

Many schools, particularly the High Mowing School, New Hampshire, and the Waldorf School of Garden City, New York, provided me with self-published materials. Beulah Emmet (undated), a founder of the High Mowing School, wrote a history of the school that provides much information and a great story. The Waldorf School of Garden City was associated for many years with the Myrin Institute for Adult Education, a non-profit organization that printed much commentary valuable in interpreting the second generation of schools in the United States, "The Americans." The school briefly had its own press, "Waldorf Press," and published John Gardner's book, *The Experience of Knowledge* (1975), also useful in constructing a picture of this second generation.

Books

I construct part of the history I wish to write by examining four books that represent the four generations of schools I have examined. I take these books to be primary sources in the sense that they reflect, without mediation, the times in which they were written. What they have to say about Waldorf schools and Steiner's educational methods reveals what the authors believed at that time. Changes among the focuses and concerns of these books reveal historical changes from, say, John Gardner's (1976) sense of Waldorf schools in the Cold War to M.C. Richards's (1980) sense of Waldorf schools as a manifestation of a "new age consciousness."

Oral History

Oral history interviews provided appropriate sources for much of this history, most especially "The Social Missionaries." The history of Waldorf schools in the United States covers less than a century, so representatives of each generation still survive. Also, except for minutes of faculty and board meetings, documentation of the day-to-day history of Waldorf schools is scanty. Especially in their early, hectic, activist years, schools produce little documentation of their own histories. Minutes for faculty and board meetings of the Rudolf Steiner School, New York City, for example, begin in 1930, the third year of the existence of the school. It is possible that someone, somewhere, has minutes from earlier meetings, but they are not part of the school's archive.

Such minutes are, unfortunately, especially poor at crucial times in the life of a school. Because of my affiliations with two schools, the Waldorf School of Garden City, New York, and the Rudolf Steiner School of Great Barrington, Massachusetts, I was able to examine minutes from periods of crisis in each school. In Garden City, I read through minutes of meetings around the time that John Gardner, then director of the Waldorf Institute (a teacher education program of Adelphi University) was asked to resign.

In Great Barrington, I read through meeting minutes around the time that the school had to close a high school that it had started four years earlier. Both of these events were traumatic, and both are conspicuous in their absence from official minutes. Discussions were clearly "off the record." Interviewing those present for these events, however, recaptures the intensity of feeling surrounding the events, and allows different versions of the same event (not an officially recorded one) to be heard.

This point illustrates, however, a weakness of oral history. People remember events differently and fallibly. The best I could do was interview several people who expressed different accounts of the same events; attempt to locate self-published or recorded accounts of the events; and attempt to interpolate a coherent narrative where possible, making note of conflicting stories and differing memories.

There is a sense, of course, in which my narrative, sketchy as it is, is as fallible and different from other possible narratives as those of the people I interviewed. But clearly there is also value in the reflection and interpretation made possible by historical inquiry. As long as oral histories are not taken as the last word on a topic, at best they provide detail, immediacy, and knowledge that would otherwise be opaque to history.

Also, people live their lives according to their memories, even when these are faulty or factually wrong. As Alessandro Portelli makes clear, the importance of memory as recovered by oral history "lies... in the fact that it [becomes] the ground upon which collective memory and imagination [build] a cluster of tales, symbols, legends, and imaginary reconstructions." (1991, 1) He refers to the death of an Italian laborer in 1949 in Terni that, by the 1980s, was remembered as having occurred during labor riots in 1953. Newspaper accounts offered historically accurate accounts of Trastulli's death and of the labor riots four years later, but the people of Terni had conflated two events that occurred years apart. I did not come across such wild disparities in my own research, although stories relating a crisis at the Waldorf School of Garden City, New York, show a wide range of memory and subsequent interpretation. I struggled with this, as with other oral historical evidence, to make it clear when facts are facts, and when interpretations have provided the basis for belief and action, but have not necessarily been established as fact.

Generations

My primary finding regarding the history of Waldorf schools in the United States is that this history may be divided into roughly four generations. The first of these is "The Europeans," lasting from 1928 until roughly World War II. It contains only one surviving school, the Rudolf Steiner School in New York City, and is characterized by the transmission and translation to the United States of educational methods that had originated in Europe. Many of the people associated with the founding and teaching at this first school were German or Swiss, and many of the issues the school faced had to do with its relationship to a European method of education.

The second generation, "The Americans," begins during World War II with the founding of the High Mowing School in New Hampshire, and ends roughly with the re-founding of the Sacramento, California, school in 1965. It contains half a dozen schools, and sees the spread of Waldorf schools to the West Coast. It is characterized by a concern to re-make Steiner's method and curriculum for American students and families.

I initially toyed with a further distinction, dividing a third "countercultural" generation of the 1960s and early 1970s from a later "new age" generation. I came to believe strongly, however, that the concerns of the counterculture, as found in the founders of and teachers in Waldorf schools, were not significantly different from those of the "new age." It became more expedient and, I believe, more accurate, to think of them as early and later phases of the same phenomenon, a "turning away" from perceived "mainstream" or "established" culture. Hence, I have called this third generation "The Alternatives."

In this, I subscribe to a relatively conservative view of the period I am studying. As David Farber (1994) put it:

> For more and more Americans... experience itself was relegated to new, less traditionally and collectively grounded meanings [from approximately 1950 through the late 1980s]. Active and equitable participation in work life and community life were exchanged, or at least refigured, for consumption opportunities and demands for more consumption opportunities. (307)

A fourth generation may be discerned among some schools founded beginning in the early 1990s, characterized by an unwillingness to make the same compromises that previous generations had made. All three previous generations consist of independent or private schools; these schools charge tuition and therefore draw from a relatively elite pool of students and families. Schools like the Milwaukee Urban Waldorf School, Wisconsin, a public Waldorf school, and the Wolakota Waldorf School, South Dakota, an externally-funded free school on the Pine Ridge Reservation, are willing to make other compromises—with the "purity" of their curriculum, for example—in order to serve different constituents. These schools, and charter Waldorf schools on the West Coast, for example, constitute a new way of thinking about Waldorf education, and hence constitute a fourth generation. I call this generation "The Social Missionaries" for its central attempt to bring Waldorf education to students who are not served by independent schools.

Generations

Positing different generations raises the question of transitions from one to the next. To use an evolutionary metaphor, we could ask what changes in the environment produce an adaptive response that we may characterize as a generational change?

Here, Waldorf schools must be seen as embedded in their times. To find a European influence before World War II, and a greater focus on American interests afterward, can hardly be a surprise, for example. But there also appear to be internal spurs to the changes I describe, changes more like those found in a family. Junior grows up and seeks to differentiate himself from his parents. In this regard, the history of Waldorf schools in the United States is a family saga. Momma and Poppa arrive from the Old World, certain of their values but seeking to fit in. They scrape by. Their children speak English as a first language, although they can still talk with Grandma in the old tongue if necessary. They try to persuade the old folks of the value of new ways, and work to be really American. Their own children rebel against their bourgeois striving to fit in, and leave to do their own thing. They start communes, seek alternative lifestyles. The older generations wish they would listen and learn, but they won't, for the most part, and have to invent things for themselves. Their own children find this rebellion and alternative-seeking quaint, and seek to do some practical good in the world. They're still trying to find their way. And, in a nutshell, that's the history I found.

Having posited four generations of Waldorf schools in the United States, I will write that an equally valid, if perhaps not so interesting, history could be written that emphasizes the continuity and similarity of Waldorf schools across time, that attempts to dismantle the notion of generational change. To emphasize continuity or similarity, however, promotes the idea that Waldorf schools are one thing when they are many. Even given their similarities, and given their continuity, Waldorf schools have changed over time, and it is worthwhile to explain this change coherently. The idea of generations has helped me to do this.

Chronology and Geography

Part of my research has been to determine the chronology, growth, number, and location of Waldorf schools in the United

States. I believe I have been relatively successful in this, discovering significantly more Waldorf schools than I initially supposed there were (and many more than the Association of Waldorf Schools of North America recognizes or tracks).

Child's Play

Although I deny that Waldorf education exists as an object, it is still possible to characterize the ideas and practices of teachers in Waldorf schools, ideas and practices that cannot presently be found in similar configurations in other schools today. I aim to pursue this discussion in the most general way; this essay is not a primer in Waldorf education, and readers may find any number of helpful distillations of Steiner's ideas on education. (I recommend particularly Steiner's *The Education of the Child in the Light of Anthroposophy* [available in *The Education of the Child* (1996a)]; Barnes's "An Introduction to Waldorf Education"; and Harwood's *The Recovery of Man in Childhood*.)

As one example, I will focus here on the importance of play and tacit knowing in Waldorf schools. I could give equal consideration to the importance of aesthetics and imagination, and to the importance of empiricism and wholeness. These are qualities that become apparent on visiting schools or reading the literature of Waldorf education. The importance of play and tacit knowing, however, are perhaps the least familiar, and consequently potentially the most illuminating. In Waldorf schools, play and tacit knowing concern primarily the education of preschool children. Aesthetics concerns primarily the education of elementary school children, and the development of thinking, high school children.

These ideas provide touchstones that lie beneath the education of children at each of roughly three stages of development, but each is present throughout life. Looking forward in the life of a child, we cannot deny that imagination and intellect are present even in the youngest, albeit in prototype and in a relatively unconscious, undeveloped form. Teachers' focus at the younger ages is on doing, on play, on imitation, with the future development of conscious imagination and conscious intellect in mind.

And, looking back through the development of school-age children, we do not see play or imitation evaporate to be replaced by imagination. Steiner's stage description is cumulative. It is also truly developmental. The unconscious imitation of young children's play may evolve into both a quick-witted ability consciously to imitate others, and into an inner, imaginative, even moral imitative sense (where previously imitation consisted primarily of externalized copying).

These three ways of knowing (Waldorf schools frequently speak of "thinking, feeling, and willing") underlie many of the techniques of the Waldorf school method. The first of these, the importance of play, accords with what Michael Polanyi has called "tacit knowing." (1983) The second accords with an imaginative understanding of, or knowledge about, the world. And the third provides the ground of experience for an intellectual understanding of the world.

Play and Tacit Knowing

Separate from the discussions of Waldorf teachers about the importance of imaginative play for young children, Sara Smilansky (1990) developed a large body of research over four decades supporting the importance of what she calls "sociodramatic play" for young children. Among her conclusions are the following:

- Improving dramatic and sociodramatic play improves cognitive and socio-emotional skills (225).
- "Sociodramatic play," "free play," "doll play," "make-believe play" should be included as a central element in the daily schedule of the preschool and kindergarten curriculum. All children in the classroom should be invited from time to time (at least twice a week) to participate in pretend play, indoors and outdoors, with clearly declared expectations

that they will cooperate with others and engage in enacting a theme for a certain period of time (229).

- The natural tendency of young children for imitation and pretense, even if manifested on the most concrete level, offers a unique opportunity for enrichment and growth while building on processes from within (231).

Smilansky, a developmental psychologist, does not offer philosophical support for her findings, but it seems clear that a good part of the effectiveness of the play she describes is in its contribution to what Michael Polanyi calls "tacit knowledge"; that is, the idea that *"we can know more than we can tell."* (1983, 4; italics in original.) This may sound like a platitude, but its implications are profound: Tacit knowing "brings home to us that it is not by looking at things, but by dwelling in them, that we understand their joint meaning" (18). And what is Smilansky's sociodramatic play if not an imaginative "dwelling in"?

Tacit knowing, knowing more than we can tell, includes as well our perception of truth; that is, "when a discovery solves a problem" (a problem that cannot be recognized explicitly, only tacitly, because its solution is unknown until discovered), "its truth as a solution can be recognized but not known explicitly" (23). You and I can agree on a truth, can know it together; but, short of your recognition, there is nothing I can do to convince you of its truth or inculcate it in or inject it into you. Formal geometric proofs constitute the clearest examples in this category of knowing. The experience of their truth extends the idea of empiricism, for example, beyond the notion of common sensory experience.

Hence, the importance of tacit knowing, I believe, illustrates the real value of transcendence. I can demonstrate the congruence of two triangles, for example, by showing you that two sides and the included angle are equal in measure. But I cannot recognize the truth of this congruence for you. By attending to the configuration before you, and the concepts that this configuration represents, either you will intuitively recognize this truth, or you won't. And if you do, nothing short of brain damage can undo this recognition; you have transcended your prior understanding of the world, and it now includes a truth of which you were previously unaware, and of which you can speak only with reference to particulars that may lead another to the same recognition of truth.

Tacit knowing is first knowing. Young children play, and their play develops in them far-reaching possibilities for recognizing or attending to truths unknown, as individuals and, simultaneously, as members of a community.

PART 1

The HISTORY of
WALDORF EDUCATION
in the UNITED STATES

1. THE EUROPEANS

ON THE UPPER EAST SIDE OF MANHATTAN, in one of the most exclusive neighborhoods in the world, sits the Rudolf Steiner School, the first Waldorf or Steiner school in the United States. It inhabits two buildings on East Seventy-Eighth and East Seventy-Ninth Streets, just in from Fifth Avenue, a couple of blocks south of the sprawling beaux arts Metropolitan Museum of Art on Museum Mile. On Seventy-Ninth Street, the school is next to the home of the billionaire mayor of New York City, Michael Bloomberg. Leaving the school in the late afternoon, I saw that the regular detail of New York City police on the sidewalk had increased to half a dozen. As I chatted with some students, a large black SUV pulled to the curb, and Bloomberg emerged with a couple of bodyguards. They and the mayor gave us a "once-over," and he entered his building. Bloomberg is shorter than average, and he left the impression of a Campbell's condensed version of astuteness, self-possession, and power.

During the school day children (younger ones holding on to a length of rope, led by their teacher) troop across Fifth Avenue to play in Central Park. On the sidewalks, older students appear and depart, chattering and at home in a city that easily makes out-of-towners feel a bit lost.

Inside, the school feels cramped to someone from outside the City; small, high-ceilinged classrooms and narrow hallways, stairwells, and bathrooms. Much has been updated in a non-descript style, but here and there remnants of the grand old buildings remain—marble floors, a fireplace, paneling. Like other such schools (Dalton, Trinity), despite wealth and prestige, the buildings feel like warrens or hives when full; each student, teacher, parent, and administrator busy, on schedule and on task, navigating through the labyrinths of a school configured inside buildings that were not designed as school buildings.

For more than a decade, from 1928 until 1941 or 1942 or so, the Rudolf Steiner School was just about the only Waldorf school in the United States. The first generation of schools in the United States, then, is represented only by this first school. Its influence on other schools, directly through the development of practices and curriculum, and indirectly through the training of teachers who ended up virtually everywhere in the United States, is undeniable.

I say "just about the only school" because at least one other school was founded but failed during this period; that was a small school founded by Roger and Marion Hale in Vanceboro, Maine, in the late 1930s. And at least two other schools that later became successful Waldorf schools existed and experimented with "Waldorf" methods during this period. These were The Edgewood School in Greenwich, Connecticut, which moved to Wilton, New Hampshire, in 1941, and changed its name to the High Mowing School, and the Highland Hall School in Los Angeles, which became, by its own definition, a Waldorf school in 1955. These schools differ from the Steiner School in New York City in that they existed as conventional independent schools first, and adopted Waldorf methods and curricula later; the Steiner School was founded by a group of anthroposophists, the Rudolf Steiner Educational Union, to put Steiner's educational ideas into practice. By postponing their plunge into Waldorf education until World War II and later, the other schools inadvertently assured that their early histories would fall more in the generation I have termed "The Americans."

Because of the kindness of Lucy Schneider, then Faculty Chair at the Steiner School, and of the Steiner School's College of Teachers, I had access to the school's complete archive of faculty meeting minutes from 1930 to 1950. These included weekly faculty meeting and monthly joint faculty-board meeting minutes. Although Ms. Schneider claimed there should be minutes from the start of the school in 1928 or 1929, I found only those beginning in 1930. These minutes provide an invaluable record of the day-to-day operation of the school, its longer-term concerns, and its relationships with other independent schools in New York; with Waldorf schools in Europe; and with the

Anthroposophical Society in general. Also, through approximately 1943, the school made a practice of attaching important correspondence received (and replies sent) during a given week to the faculty meeting minutes for that week, providing another valuable link with the past. Finally, copies of important documents like budget projections and publicity pamphlets were inserted into the minute books, as well.

Founding

The founding date of the Rudolf Steiner School depends on whom you consult and what criterion you choose. The school today dates itself to 1928. That was the year of the founding of the Rudolf Steiner Educational Union (now the Rudolf Steiner Educational Foundation), and the date that the first thirteen students met in Irene Brown's apartment at 111 East Thirty-Ninth Street in the Murray Hill neighborhood of New York.

The beginning of the Rudolf Steiner School in New York was extremely modest. Instituted primarily through the generosity of an enthusiastic and generous woman, Miss Irene Brown, it began with two teachers and enrolled during the first year, 1928, only 13 pupils. The following year a suitable building at 20 W. 73 Street, which was being vacated by The Dalton School, was leased, and the new school enrolled 33 pupils. (From an undated "annual report"-style typescript, author unknown, 12 pp., with an estimated budget for 1939-1940, hence most likely from spring, 1939).

Henry Barnes, former faculty chair of the Steiner School, describes Irene Brown as a "tall, distinguished, reserved" woman, one who met Rudolf Steiner several times and resolved to bring his work to the United States. She was not only responsible, with others, for founding the Steiner School; she introduced other Americans to eurythmy, Steiner's art of movement, and encouraged Christoph Linder, a Swiss medical doctor, to establish a practice in anthroposophic medicine in New York City. (According to Peter Hinderberger, M.D., "Based on Rudolf Steiner's work, anthroposophic medicine includes mainstream allopathic practices, and extends them with complementary, individual-ized, and human-centered medicine.")

The world of New York education was smaller in the 1930s. Dal-ton School founder Helen Parkhurst, for instance, attended Steiner's lectures on education in England in the 1920s. We don't know what she made of them, but her school and the Steiner School were both founded in what we now often call the Progressive Era, and were both dedicated to new, progressive, and experimental education methods. Schools were smaller then, especially private schools. Choate, for exam-ple, enrolled all of six students in 1896, its first year; and similar enroll-ments—a handful of students, a house or a farm (or a living room), and a couple of teachers, were standard fare through the early part of the twentieth century.

A pamphlet produced by the Rudolf Steiner Educational Union in April 1929 announces "Paintings and Drawings Done by Children of the Waldorf School, Stuttgart, Germany, exhibited under the Auspices of the American Federation of the Arts at the Art Center, 65 E. 56th St., April 1 – 15, 1929. The method of teaching painting to children briefly described above may be seen in a very small school conducted by Mrs. Virginia Field Birdsall at 111 E. 39th Street."

Hermann von Baravalle, a colleague of Steiner in the first Waldorf School in Stuttgart, Germany, and a renowned mathematics teacher, in an undated letter most likely from 1941, wrote "In October, 1929, the Rudolf Steiner School for Boys and Girls was opened at 20 West Seventy-Third Street, New York City." That was the year the school was incorporated.

Similarly, a brochure produced by The Rudolf Steiner Educational Union, at a new address (20 W. Seventy-Third St., NYC) Vol. III, Nos. 1–2, January–April 1930, says: "As we draw near the close of the second term of our school, we look back with profound satisfaction to what has been achieved during this year. More than twice as many children have been entrusted to our care as during the first year" (1). So Baravalle is not alone in those early days, in thinking of the school as beginning in 1929.

A pamphlet, reprinted from the "Rudolf Steiner School Quarterly," January–April 1928: "Rudolf Steiner: An Introduction to His Life and Thought" by Olin D. Wannamaker, on the other hand, makes no mention of a school but includes the intention to found one. "It is our purpose to set before American parents and teachers as widely as is possible that which we consider the wisest and profoundest educational philosophy of the present age" (21). It seems that as late as April 1928 it was not certain that a school would open its doors that fall.

I spoke with Swain Pratt, however, who was a student in Irene Brown's living room in 1928, and who then moved with the Steiner School as it changed buildings. For him, there was no question that 1928 is the proper year for the school's founding, and he remembers the excitement of the new school.

The school started in the fall of 1928 as a "home school," although no one at that time would have used that phrase to describe it; and only became incorporated and institutionalized, (with grades 1 to 4) in the fall of 1929. The school year frequently began in October in those days. October 1929. Could there have been a less auspicious month in which to start a private school, or to celebrate the first birthday of a very small school initiative?

Themes

As I examined the Steiner School's archive, several themes, which I detail below, became obvious. Some arise from the sharp differences between then and now; some because of surprising similarities between then and now; and some from historical imperative. One would simply be remiss in describing events in New York City in the middle of the twentieth century without including consideration of the depression of the 1930s, World War II, or the treatment of Jews, for example. The accounts of the themes investigated below are supplemented by interviews with Lucy Schneider, then faculty chair of the school, and Henry Barnes, longtime teacher and faculty chair.

The themes evident in an account of the early years of the Steiner School can be phrased as questions, questions that were not necessarily phrased as such at the time, but that clearly informed discourse at the school. The first and most important of these, perhaps, is this: Was the school to be a copy of a German or central European school or method of education, or an interpretation of this source for a specifically American, a New York, situation? Largely because of the importance of this question to the school, I have chosen to characterize this period of the history of Waldorf schools in the United States as the period of "The Europeans." In examining its European origins, the school, and Waldorf education in the United States generally, moved toward becoming American.

German or American

Because several teachers at the school had been born in Germany or in German-speaking countries, and because several of the Americans had traveled to Germany or Switzerland for teacher training, "Germanisms" abound in the early life of the school. Throughout the 1930s, for example, many minutes begin with a phrase such as, "the meeting opened with a *Spruch* or *Sprüch.*" Why not say "verse," or "speech exercise"? On January 21, 1931, it was decided that "Mrs. Wallace will take the *Heil-eurythmy.*" *Heil* translates literally as "health" and here is better translated as "curative" or "therapeutic." The first use of "curative eurythmy" instead of "*heil* eurythmy" was not recorded until April 26, 1937. On February 2, 1940, George O'Neil, writing from Switzerland to Miss Peckham, faculty secretary at the Steiner School, about obtaining reproductions or lantern slides of Waldorf School students' work for publicity purposes, refers to "*Anschauungs* Material." *Anschauung* means "view," and we might better speak of promotional material. Finally, as late as the start of the school year in the fall of 1940, students and teachers spoke an untranslated German grace in the lunchroom.

German culture presented more than a touchstone, however, for those finding their way with this new way of teaching. It presented specific pedagogical and curricular challenges. On December 7, 1936, for example, Miss Dreher... "explained the difficulty of picturing the vowels in English and showed first her solution to this difficulty." In German, "I" is pronounced "ee," and the accompanying eurythmy gesture for this sound would be attached to the letter "E", but only for its long phoneme. More difficult, the letter "A" in English may be pronounced as in "father" or as in "make." This second pronunciation is connected with the German letter "E." The gestures of eurythmy pertain to sound and not to picture. Hence Miss Dreher's difficulties. I have not found her solution. What was clear and evident in German—one letter, one sound, one gesture—became a matter for interpretation and "solution of difficulties" in English.

Further, of course, German schools taught German literature. Were American schools also to teach Schiller and Goethe (as some still do)? Or were Shakespeare and Emerson, for example, adequate or appropriate substitutions?

As obvious as the German cultural heritage of the school was, it was never uncontested. The Germans pushed for change or consideration, more often, while the native English speakers seemed reluctant to do so. On January 28, 1931, for example, Mr. Neuscheller, a teacher and native German speaker, said it was "impossible to teach exactly the same as in the Waldorf School [in Stuttgart]. Pedagogy is necessarily different in the West." Several years later, on January 20, 1938, Hermann von Baravalle, who had taught at the original Waldorf School in Stuttgart, visited: "Do away with every intention to copy [the] Waldorf School [in Stuttgart]. What can teachers here [in America] do with what they have? Let the school grow on this soil—with roots in this soil.... Many things that are worked out here [in the West] are the future for Central Europe." And on February 2 he continued: "[It is] fundamental to build an institution to serve a situation [in New York], not reproduce a situation [in Stuttgart, that is]."

At several points over the years, the question of hiring a director or principal was broached, often by the board of directors (trustees). Almost always, the proposed candidate was not someone born in the United States. On January 15, 1936, Hermann von Baravalle himself was proposed as principal of the school (without his knowledge at first). At least one member of the faculty objected that it was "unwise to have a foreign principal in an American school." Other objections were also raised, but oddly perhaps, none on principle. (See "Governance" below.) Dr. von Baravalle declined employment at the school, although he was a friendly and frequent visitor. Little more than a year later, on March 8, 1937, the idea of a director was proposed again. Given that three teachers were leaving at the end of the school year (John and Carol Gardner and Marjorie Spock), the directors spoke of a plan to include Dr. von Baravalle unless he was engaged by the Greenwich, Connecticut, school (Edgewood School, later moved to Wilton, New

Hampshire, as the High Mowing school), or to hire a new teacher, "possibly a middle European of good training who would come in as a main class teacher and perhaps someday become principal." "Mr. Gardner suggested that any such person who was to knit the faculty together as a leader should be an American." Five teachers expressed a desire to see the American Henry Barnes in that position. He was not to arrive at the school, however, until 1940.

Again, on February 16, 1939, "The board had thought of [Dr. Schwebsch] being director or headmaster of the school…"

Both von Baravalle and Schwebsch had taught at the original Waldorf school in Stuttgart, and this apparently gave them an imprimatur that an American simply could not have; they had been hand-picked by Rudolf Steiner himself. Whether or not they were capable of directing a school, especially an American school, seems to have been little considered, at least by the board. In the interim, Margaret Pratt, an American, was hired as acting principal. In the years of the Steiner School's existence, so far as I can conclude, of approximately six faculty chairs only William Harrer was not born in the United States.

The school had to contend with questions of its American identity in addition to wrestling with its German origin. The faculty meeting of December 2, 1935, noted that

> Mrs. [S] had inquired whether the pledge to the flag might not be used in the School. A discussion of this point ensued, with the result that the Faculty felt it inadvisable to institute the pledge on principle, since young children cannot connect any reality with such a pledge. The Faculty agreed to consider and make proposals as to how a real concept of Americanism could be [fostered].

What these proposals were, and whether or not they were instituted, I cannot discover.

At least one of the school's neighbors saw the school as a European, even German school. A postcard from her, one in a series, is worth quoting here in full: "January 18, 1943. Better learn the use of the American flag! The Stars and Stripes are not to be flown in the rain, all day, bedraggled into soaking wet, even to help along a german [sic] school! Instruct your porter! [signed] American." Another postcard from the same woman, protesting children roller-skating in front of the building, was signed "Goethe."

Henry Barnes (1998) remembers ongoing decisions and challenges regarding the school's German reputation:

> During the War [World War II], to be a school that bore the name Rudolf Steiner, half the population thought you were German and therefore enemy, the other half thought you were Jewish and therefore questionable. There were many parents at that time who tried to persuade us to change our name.

Finally, Lucy Schneider (1999), who has been at the school only since 1978 or 1979, made it clear that the shadow of the past is omnipresent. She described believing, for example, that

> everybody here spoke German when I first came, and so that was a big surprise to me to discover that everybody didn't. I really thought all the class teachers had to know German, and that [belief] persists still [among some newcomers to the school].
>
> I was walking down 79th Street with Irene Mantel and Bob Dandrew and some woman comes out of a building dangling keys in front of our faces, and says, "Could one of you Germans help me? I can't get the trunk of my Mercedes open." I could not believe it. So I said, "We have a handyman—from Ireland—who's quite mechanically oriented and I'd be happy to have him help you." ... She saw us walking out of the school and that should make us good at opening a Mercedes' trunk.

Isolation or Participation?

Another struggle evident through the early years, one still relevant to those working in Waldorf schools today, is the question of the school's role in society. Is the school to be relatively cloistered or isolated, "against" the culture of the dominant society around it? Or is it to be an active participant in effecting change or reform? Minutes of a faculty meeting on May 9, 1933, put the question most simply: "Is the school part of society?"

For reasons of publicity, of course, the school had to represent itself broadly. Yet its efforts show some ambivalence. On January 4, 1931, minutes record that "Mr. Guenther knows someone on the *The New York Times* who could get an article about the school printed/published. This would be satisfactory if such an article could be printed exactly as submitted." Such an article does not exist. The school was on the lookout, however, for opportunities for publicity. On May 22, 1933, minutes record that "Radoslavovitch of NYU recommends Steiner pedagogy."

The school was also an active participant in the progressivism of the 1930s, which, it should be noted, is a somewhat chastened independent school version of earlier efforts to reform public schools. A letter from December, 1932, from the Schools Committee of the Child Study Association of America regarding a "Winter Project" on "social and international attitudes" makes clear the school's participation—as do repeated references to Child Study Association meetings, conferences, and election or appointment of Steiner school representatives; Mrs. Dennett on October 7, 1935, for example. The school was also a member of the Progressive Education Association through the 1930s. Minutes contain several references to school preparations to include children's artwork in a "showing of paintings by American children from progressive schools" by the Associated Experimental Schools (City and Country School, Hessian Hills, Little Red Schoolhouse, Manumit School, Bank Street Schools, and Walden School). Minutes from November 10, 1938, refer to attendance at a PEA meeting, a Child Study Association talk on radio to be held on December 7 at 2 p.m., and a letter to Colby College, Maine, on the use of "color" according to Steiner's pedagogy.

On March 1, 1939, mention is made of a National Child Welfare Association series on Rudolf Steiner education, to be held Saturday, March 10, from 10 a.m. to 1 p.m. A year later, on February 13, a lecture by Dr. von Baravalle on John Dewey, "where he has good ideas and how Dr. Steiner supplies his lacks," to be delivered on February 28, is mentioned. Later that spring, on May 28, 1940, the school recommends asking Dr. von Baravalle to speak at the "Progressive School Association conference to be held Nov. 29 and 30." Dr. Poppelbaum, visiting from Germany on May 13, 1941, further emphasizes the importance of what is now called "outreach": "the school should be represented at all educational conferences and meetings."

There is a strong sense throughout these early years that people believed that significant reform across American education was possible. The Steiner school could be a model for educational reform. In fact, when other schools were too similar (the Dalton School is mentioned in this regard), this was seen as something of a threat. If the difference between Steiner's ideas on education and others was not obvious enough, the school's message was in danger of becoming diluted.

Relationship to the Anthroposophical Society

Is a Waldorf school an anthroposophic institution? That is, does it exist to manifest and further the aims of an anthroposophic understanding of the world? Or does it simply gather insight into the education of children from anthroposophic research, but stand independently?

Minutes from March 27, 1933, tell us that "Mr. Monges asked for a report of the School to be made at the annual meeting at Headquarters." Mr. Monges was General Secretary of the Anthroposophical Society's New York Branch, and its location was referred to as "Headquarters." This designation reveals an attitude toward anthroposophy that is more reform-oriented than many or most of today's more isolationist Waldorf schools. Activists and reformers require a headquarters; others, perhaps, a cloister. The distinction is one of attitude: Will we take our message to the people, or will we set an example that will lead people to seek us? This is a perennial question for religious movements, and its continued strength among anthroposophists demonstrates a common misunderstanding of anthroposophy as a sect or worldview, instead of as an objective method of knowing the world.

In the early days of the Steiner School the relationship of the school to the Anthroposophical Society was strong. The school had been founded by a group of anthroposophists, and it didn't seem to occur to them, at first, that there even existed a question of the school's independence from the Anthroposophical Society. On May 9, 1933, minutes record that "Mr. Wannamaker moved that members of the board and the faculty appoint a Committee to take steps that may seem practicable to bring about the best cooperation between the members of the different groups of the Society and members at large on the one hand, and the school on the other, in order to make the school thoroughly a part of the [Anthroposophical] Society in America."

That fall (of 1933), an international hullabaloo arose regarding a breach of confidentiality with regard to statements about a German Steiner school made at the New York school. Letters were sent to and from Frau Marie Steiner, Dr. Steiner's wife, and the "Vorstand" or leadership of the international Anthroposophical Society, attempting to sort out the hurt feelings and ideological issues.

Because of this ongoing discussion, however, Marjorie Spock, a teacher at the school and sister of the famous Dr. Benjamin Spock, wrote a letter to the rest of the faculty on November 7, 1933, questioning requests for confidentiality regarding decidedly non-pedagogical, non-school related business. "Such secrecy [regarding what she considered gossip behind closed doors] limits individual initiative and responsibility and puts an unnatural check on moral freedom. Doing away with such secrecy need in no way curtail openness and cordiality among faculty members. On the contrary, it stimulates a regard for fairness, exactness, and responsibility of utterance." Her letter indicates the beginning of a recognition that school business and anthroposophic business were not or need not be healthfully intertwined. Still, throughout the 1930s, the Steiner School sent annual telegrams to Marie Steiner on her birthday. (See minutes from March 1936, 1937, and 1942).

Later in the 1930s, questions regarding the potential separation of the school and the society become more frequent. On January 20, 1938, Hermann von Baravalle, visiting the school, said, "There is no such thing as an Anthroposophical school." Minutes from May 31, 1939, record that "Some feel that the school should not be associated with Anthroposophy in the public mind." Presumably, a private relationship is still taken for granted. On June 12, 1939, "It is thought that it would be better not to combine with HQ [headquarters of the New York City branch of the Anthroposophical Society] because of the association in the public mind of the school with something sectarian and occult."

Those familiar with Waldorf schools today will recognize the difficulties of sorting out an appropriate relationship with the Anthroposophical Society, although the sense that a school is one member of a larger effort at social reform, an effort that has an HQ, may seem quaint. Does this mean such efforts are presently more covert, or that twenty-first century Americans are somewhat chastened with regard to hopes for societal reform?

Is the Steiner School a Christian School?

Of somewhat less pressing importance but still manifest in the school's archive is the question of the school's relationship to Christianity. Given its German heritage and the rise of national socialism in Germany during the 1930s, the question of the school's relationship to Jews also surfaces from time to time. Such sensitive matters are represented only sketchily in the minutes, and researchers must be careful not to read too much into the bits that are present.

On November 21, 1932, "Jewish parents asked permission for their children to take part in [the] Christmas play." That they needed to ask indicates that there was at least the possibility that their children might otherwise be excluded. But whether this exclusion would be due to a feeling that only Christians should participate, or that Jews might be offended if included, is not clear.

On May 24, 1937, minutes record the application of a boy who might present a problem: "We are willing to accept [O] if he will study hard, be here on time, miss only when ill, express no feeling against Jews..."

These two entries, however slight, indicate a sensitivity to appropriate feelings between Christians and Jews. As the 1930s progressed, however, the school didn't always acquit itself so well. Two Jewish refugees applied to the school in November, 1938, but their admittance "would overbalance the percent of Jewish children," according to at least one teacher (November 17, 1938). Nonetheless, they were admitted by December 1, and their tuition was paid by a friend of the school, provided they could raise money for "carfare and supplies."

On January 12, 1939, one proposed book (a reader?) of Old Testament stories, part of the third grade curriculum, was considered "too Jewish" to adopt. We may well ask, why?

And on October 4, 1939, at least one teacher went on record, saying, "As a Christian school we have to be careful about the percentage of Jewish children." This question—is a Waldorf school a Christian school?—is still cause for unease and dissent among Waldorf teachers today. One parent with whom I spoke, a highly educated man, a Jew, and a trained Waldorf teacher, who believes Waldorf schools are appropriately nonsectarian, was told during an interview for his children at the Steiner School in New York City that he was applying to a Christian school. This occurred in the 1980s.

Other Steiner Schools

The evidence is slim, but it seems the Steiner School cast relationships with other Waldorf schools in a three-tiered hierarchy. At the top was the model, the original Waldorf School in Stuttgart, from which several teachers and consultants came to New York. In the middle were existing Waldorf schools in other countries, especially, for example, in England. "Miss Peckham will write to Helen Fox at the English school, asking about English translation[s] of lectures Dr. Steiner gave to Waldorf School teachers" (October 27, 1930). Or, seeking ways to raise money and generate interest: "[We should send a] letter to all Rudolf Steiner schools in Europe asking for information about their schools" (January 25, 1937).

At the bottom were, as they were founded, other Waldorf schools in North America. For example, on May 28, 1940, "Mrs. DeSylva, a Mexican, is in New York and plans to start a Rudolf Steiner School in Mexico. Schools professing to teach our pedagogy should be our responsibility." Remember that the Stuttgart school was closed during this time. Or, on September 24, 1941: "Dr. Hiebel visited Los Angeles [Highland Hall] over the summer. The school has eurythmy and painting but 'it isn't a real Waldorf school.'"

This is not to say that the school wasn't supportive and delighted as other schools came into being, and as other persons became interested in Waldorf education. January 4, 1931, for example, saw the beginning of a long relationship between the Hales of Boston and the Steiner School:

Mrs. Roger Hale, friend of Miss Brown, took her child, who is subnormal, to Arlesheim [location of a Swiss anthroposophical medical clinic]. She is so much interested in the work and so enthusiastic that she desires to start a school in Boston. She wants to make a study of the methods from Kindergarten on of the entire idea. It was suggested that she do her own reading, asking questions and getting inspiration when she makes her visits to New York.

January 7, 1931: "Mrs. Birdsall spoke again of Mrs. Hale. She wants the teachers to plan a correspondence course for her. It was suggested that the first step be General Pedagogy. She should read and when she comes to New York discuss her questions. These will be answered from knowledge of more intimate lectures. Mr. Neuscheller suggested that she come here for a conference in order to know what she knows and wants to learn."

The school's association with the Hales continued. In 1932 they were voted "Founder Members" of the school. In addition to their residence in Boston, they owned Sunrise Farm in Vanceboro, Maine, where they attempted to start a school. This venture is delightfully outlined in the memoir *The Education of a Yankee*, by their son, Judson Hale. Hale was, briefly, a student at the Sunrise Farm school, and then a student at the High Mowing School. Among other things, he describes a Swiss anthroposophic lecturer in a three-piece suit, up to his ankles in mud, describing esoteric anthroposophic concepts to Maine loggers. Judson Hale is the retired editor of *Yankee* magazine. A letter from Roger Hale at the farm dated December 11, 1941, promises to send greens from Maine to New York for the children of the Steiner School, presumably evergreens to decorate the school for the holidays.

As other schools, especially those involving persons known to the Steiner School, were founded, information becomes more matter-of-fact. On October 2 and October 25, 1941, the school received letters from Virginia Birdsall and Elizabeth de Grunelius at the Kimberton Farm School, Pennsylvania. Mrs. Birdsall was a founding teacher at the Steiner School, but she would now teach in Kimberton.

On April 8, 1942, the school received an announcement of the formation of the High Mowing School, the first Waldorf high school in the United States, and the only boarding Waldorf school, by Mrs. Beulah Emmet and the von Baravalles, who had been frequent visitors in New York. A later letter, on August 28, 1943, announced the first graduating class at the High Mowing School.

An Early Crisis

Present Waldorf schools may subscribe to a "Golden Age" notion of their own history, thinking that closer in time to Steiner's life and "indications," the mission and work must have been clearer. The record of the Steiner School's first years, however, shows otherwise. Challenges arose and patterns were established that have hardly changed in more than eighty years.

Teachers may believe, for example, that collegial relationships must have been more cordial in those heady early days. But minutes from March 1936 characterize difficulties between "old" and "new" "forces" on the faculty. Read "old" and "new" as code for difficulties between some older or more established teachers and two fiery younger faculty members in particular, Marjorie Spock and John Gardner, both of whom eventually resigned, and a decade later, joined the faculty of the fledgling Garden City, New York, Waldorf School. John Gardner, faculty chair at the Steiner School, announced his resignation on January 25, 1937, effective June 1 of that year. Marjorie Spock, "felt so hopeless when the outspokenness of a fearless person [Mr. Gardner] is mistaken that if there were no room for Mr. Gardner there would be no room for her." Mr. Gardner was accused of "taking himself too seriously.... After all, he had only been at the school two years." Another colleague, on the other hand, supported him by characterizing Mr. Gardner as "the yeast which most necessary [sic] fulfills its function by fomenting." Later, on Long Island, New York, actively opposing pesticide spraying, Marjorie Spock befriended a young writer, Rachel Carson, to whom Spock dedicated her book, *To Look On Earth With More Than Mortal Eyes*.

Tension in the school over these resignations is apparent in the minutes for months. April 12, 1937, records: "The business meeting was opened and minutes called for and read. Dr. Hubbard objected to the minutes on the grounds of inaccuracy—not showing a true picture. The secretary asked for specific incidents of inaccuracy and was given that of the omission of words spoken by Mr. Gardner concerning his intentions for next year. The secretary flung her book on the table and suggested that Dr. Hubbard try keeping the minutes." Three pages of minutes follow, with several violent pencil slashes through them, summarizing opinions regarding Mr. Gardner's relationship to the school.

Though officially stricken from the record, the minutes are completely legible.

Minutes of November 23, 1936, record "Questions for [a] Parent Evening." Readers familiar with contemporary Waldorf schools will recognize every one of these questions, even where the context needs to be updated slightly. Suffice it to say that the questions concern areas of difference from conventional private and public education of the time, even compared with member schools of the Progressive Education Association (PEA) on the Upper East Side of New York. Questions today are remarkably similar.

> Why not tempera instead of transparent [paint]?
> Why not typewriter?
> Why do we use fairy tales, myths and Bible stories rather than here and now stories?
> What attitude on discipline?
> Why boys how to sew and crochet?
> Why first grade at change of teeth?
> Why colored pencils used?
> Why German and French so early?
> Why start arithmetic with division?
> Why paintings in one class same in subject and arrangement?
> Do we teach religion?
> Do we have prayers?

Organization and Governance

Readers may suspect that school organization and governance were more clearly delineated or less controversial in those early days. But minutes of November 14, 1932, from a meeting of faculty and directors [trustees] record,

> While the Faculty has the right to govern the school still the Directors should be better informed especially when it concerns salaried members of the Faculty. The educational and business ends should not be so totally separate though the power of appointing and dismissing is entirely up to the Faculty.

Two weeks later, November 28, 1932, a bit of (temporary) clarity: "faculty hire and fire; executive committee members [all faculty] elected for 4 month terms."

Or not. February 15, 1933, in a report of a joint faculty-board committee: "no decision of vital importance for the Rudolf Steiner School shall be taken, without such decision being arrived at by joint action of the Board of Directors and the Faculty. This agreement naturally does not refer to any decision of purely pedagogical nature."

By March 20, 1933, perhaps frustrated by lack of leadership, minutes ask, "Should the school have an Acting Director?" The question was unresolved and became dormant for a couple of years. It resurfaced, at least in the school's minutes, on January 15, 1936, with the proposal of Hermann von Baravalle as principal of the school. Again, the question became dormant until March a year later.

March 8, 1937. Given that three teachers were leaving at the end of the academic year (Mr. and Mrs. Gardner and Miss Spock), the directors spoke of a plan to include Dr. von Baravalle unless he was engaged by the Greenwich School (The Edgewood School, later High Mowing), or to hire a new teacher, "possibly a middle European of good training who would come in as a main class teacher and perhaps someday become principal."

The discussion was tabled again until November 4, 1937, when the issue returned: whether or not the school should have a principal.

A bit over a year later, February 16, 1939, "The Board had thought of [Dr. Schwebsch] being director or headmaster of the school..." No action or further discussion is recorded for three months. Then minutes record a directive from the board to the faculty May 31, 1939: "We need a "special acting principal" [called "director" on June 12, 1939] for contact with parents and outside world."

June 7, 1939. Six years after the question first arose, Mrs. Margaret Pratt was hired as "acting principal." She has been a parent at the school since its inception. Leaders in the school previously had included Virginia Birdsall and John Gardner as "faculty chairs"; William Harrer would be faculty chair afterward, followed by Henry Barnes.

That fall saw significant discussion and clarification of faculty meeting formats (September 12, 1939): "3 types of meetings for faculty: Wed.: business–1/2 hour; child study–1 1/2 hours. Thurs.: eurythmy, then teachers' study. New teachers have no vote nor decision-making power." At the end of October (October 28, 1939) faculty meeting time was established from 3:45-6:30 pm. There is no record of whether this was an increase or decrease of previous meeting lengths, or of the possibility that it simply represented a formal expectation of those attending. Shortly afterward, Mrs. Pratt resigned because of poor health, and the school was back at square one. Minutes from March 19, 1940, record the "desirability of having a permanent Executive Committee or an acting principal." No action was recorded, however, but I believe, based on my reading of the minutes, that William Harrer acted as interim faculty chair.

The next fall, Henry Barnes's presence is noted for first time (September 20, 1940). He had returned to the United States following seven years of training and teaching in Europe, first in Switzerland and then in England. According to him (1999), he was on one of the last ships to leave for the United States before the start of World War II. A year later (September 13, 1941), Barnes was faculty chair. Except for a hiatus for military service from 1943 to 1946, (during which William Harrer was again faculty chair), Barnes's tenure lasted until 1979. During his absence, minutes ask (March 3, 1943), "Do we [the faculty] run the school? Does the Board run the school? They control us by the $ they give. We control them by leaving if we don't like it."

School Life

Amid the humdrum life of the school some items stand out for their oddness and some for their resonance with education today. Discussions regarding students were carried on in a vocabulary familiar to Waldorf teachers but not to others (with regard to a child's "etheric" or "astral" lives, for example); and also in the vocabulary of the time, a vocabulary that is today politically incorrect, to say the least. For example, on January 4, 1931, "It was decided to consider [J] backward but not subnormal. She should wear a ring made of copper wire, on both finger and pencil." (This prescription, I believe, copies one given by Steiner for a student discussed in the lectures collected as *Curative Education*.) "Backward" and "subnormal" are words that are somewhat painful to read today, but they are at least familiar. The belief in the healing power of copper is unusual but not unheard of, although why a ring on the pencil should have any effect is not explained. This reference is the only example of this practice I have found.

Teachers who assign summer reading or require class readers will find the following passage familiar [undated]: "Mrs. Birdsall suggested that the two upper grades have definite outside reading. We should have reading lists of best classics. The children should then be required to read a certain number and then make a written or oral report." Summer reading, an American educational practice, enters the world of Waldorf schools.

The following comment speaks both to the idealistic nature of the teachers' enterprise and to a slight lack of trust: "The whole faculty [four or five teachers] should be consulted when a child is to be punished" (February 26, 1933). Enrollment for this year was approximately thirty-five. Which teacher did what to elicit statement of this policy?

Waldorf schools today set themselves apart from other schools, often, by refusing to give standardized or achievement tests and by setting relatively early calendar "cut off" dates for entry into first grade. They also, especially with regard to the early grades of elementary school, resist comparison with the achievements of comparable students in other schools. They postpone formally teaching writing or reading until first and second grade, for example, and recognize that children who leave a Waldorf school in the early grades may have to play catch-up in another school. This is not to say that they are not teaching soundly with an eye toward future reading; abundant storytelling, play-acting, puppetry, engagement with the natural world, drawing and painting, and eurythmy, all help to lay a foundation for future learning, from building cultural knowledge to developing hand-eye coordination and sensory integration.

Waldorf schools find that these practices preserve valuable aspects of childhood in the face of systems that would promote too-rapid advancement and a superficial maturation (see Elkind, D., *The Hurried Child*). Waldorf school teachers, then, may be surprised by some of the decisions made by their early colleagues at the Steiner School. It may be tempting to dismiss these decisions as compromises with ideals that would ask for different decisions, but in none of the cases cited below is there any record of second thoughts, hesitation, or other indications that the decision is difficult or that it goes against established principles.

The age for first grade entrance? "6 before Christmas, but exceptions possible" (April 4, 1939). Most Waldorf schools today require students to be six already, sometimes for a few months, before they enter first grade. It is worth pointing out that Steiner referred frequently to changes that take place "in the seventh year," for example, and that the seventh year begins when a child turns six. It is possible that Waldorf schools today actually misinterpret Steiner's suggestions. And, although the effects of delaying students' entry into first grade may not at first be obvious, by the time these same students are in eighth or ninth grade and demonstrate appropriate maturation, Waldorf schools may not be structured to address their needs.

On October 7, 1935, a committee was established to find appropriate achievement tests. And later, "All classes except first [grade] to keep up to public school standards. Mr. Harrer's class (grade 4) will have achievement tests" (April 20, 1939).

"Home study" and "home work" [sic] amounts were not discussed in the minutes until 1941. "H. Barnes suggests 1 hour/night beginning in fifth grade. Mr. Harrer states that parents and teachers must be in agreement" (November 5 and 12, 1941). Most Waldorf schools today phase homework in gradually over the course of several grades, often giving little in comparison with other schools, at least until high school. It is worth noting that the issue of homework has its own history; homework was illegal in New York public schools prior to 1910, for example. And no conclusive studies demonstrate that homework raises grades or improves learning.

Waldorf schools today also take a strong stand against television, usually requesting or even requiring that children see little or none. It deadens imagination, for example, they claim. Their predecessors at the Steiner School did not have to contend with television in the early years; it had not become a commercial medium. Movies provided a ground for contention, however, and the following reference characterizes the Steiner School's response to them (October 27, 1930): "Is it acceptable to suggest a movie to children if it is of historical or geographical significance?" "Do not let children see movies: They are bad for the eyes; spoil imagination; stir up slime in human." "It was agreed

to start definite education against movies." The Steiner School joined
with other East Side private schools to prevail upon several local the-
aters to advertise family showings that omitted sensational and violent
newsreels in the 1930s.

Depression and War

The early years of the Steiner School coincide with some of the most
momentous of the twentieth century, including especially the world
depression that preceded World War II, and the war itself. The events
associated with these times must have affected the lives of those at the
school, but it is good to bear in mind that such events often find coher-
ence only in retrospect.

Minutes of the Steiner School contain surprisingly little mention of
the wider world, only occasionally noting the financial difficulties of
the times, for example; and then only in notes to the effect that teachers have agreed to take a salary reduction in order to keep the school
open. The war, too, appears only in mention of specific circumstances:
a teacher leaving for service in the armed forces; a visa to help a European come to the United States; a possible "refugee policy"; or occa-
sional mention of students helping to prepare first aid kits to be shipped
overseas.

Readers may notice that references from 1942 and 1943 are absent.
Unfortunately, minutes from these years are almost illegible. What
had been excellent practice for more than a decade (reviewing minutes for accuracy, attaching correspondence and publications) became
a researcher's tragedy. In 1944, minutes appear again in a crisp form,
this time typed, but without correspondence attached. The school had
grown and matured. Its business consequently spilled beyond the small
notebooks that contained pictures of its life during its first decade of
existence. Other schools grew, as well, and informed the generation I
will call "the Americans."

2. THE AMERICANS

WHEN HERMANN VON BARAVALLE RETURNED returned to the United States in the fall of 1937, there were two Waldorf schools on American soil: The Rudolf Steiner School in New York City, and the Hale's Sunrise Farm school in Vanceboro, Maine, which was little known and soon to close. Baravalle had been offered the directorship of the Steiner School but had declined. He quickly associated himself with the Edgewood School, in Greenwich, Connecticut, and later became instrumental in the founding of the Kimberton Farm School, Pennsylvania, and The Waldorf Demonstration School of Adelphi College, New York (now the Waldorf School of Garden City). We can only guess at his reasons for disassociating himself from the Steiner School, but among them may be a belief that the Steiner School was too "European." His remarks, cited in the last chapter, regarding establishing Waldorf schools as "American" schools may have been somewhat pointed; if people are doing things the way you believe they should, you don't have to offer an opinion on how they should be done. And Baravalle, a frequent visitor to the Steiner School previously, seems not to have visited the Steiner School from this point on. It may also be that the Rudolf Steiner School was on its feet and Baravalle wanted to be involved with founding new schools. If there are more personal reasons for his absence, they seem lost to history. In any event, Baravalle later wrote:

...I returned to the United States with the task of introducing the Waldorf School Plan into an existing American school. This was the Edgewood School in Greenwich, Connecticut. In its faculty meeting of December 15, 1937, the motion was made by the head of the high school, Dr. Maud Thompson, to accept the Waldorf School Plan throughout the Edgewood High School. The motion was carried unanimously. The Principal, Miss Euphrosyne Langley, and the President of the Trustees, Mrs. Robert H. [Beulah] Emmet, were in complete agreement. The motion called for immediate action. As it was shortly before Christmas time, the necessary work for the change was carried out during the holiday and the school re-opened in January 1938 with its new plan. This was the only time that an existing school changed over to the Waldorf School Plan in the midst of a school year. The action proved to be completely successful.... When it [the Waldorf School Plan] was taken up, both the students and the parents liked it. (1963, 18).

One of Baravelle's former students at High Mowing, Leonore Russell, remembers that "he taught geometry, and we were all struck by the way this handsome, charismatic teacher's head was a nearly perfect pentagon, with a square jaw and a point at the top."

Thus a third school in the United States, in a dramatic turn that we can only try to imagine, came to use Steiner's methods. The Edgewood School relocated to Beulah Emmet's New Hampshire farm, High Mowing, in 1942, and the High Mowing School dates its founding to that year, not to its earlier incarnation in Connecticut. The Edgewood School presumably continued to exist, although I do not know for how long, as a school that no longer employed Waldorf methods. In an unpublished history of High Mowing School, Mrs. Emmet writes,

In the spring of 1942 I said: "I will put you in my barn." This was to a group of faculty [including the head of the high school, Maud Thompson] who had resigned from the Edgewood School in Greenwich, Connecticut, out of loyalty to a principle of freedom. Since I had resigned first, there seemed to be a responsibility involved, and after all there was the farm to go to. This was in April 1942 and we quietly went on planning and building as if there were no war in Europe and no dearth of materials here. To make a farm into a school from May to October was the problem (9).

I was unable to discover what principle of freedom was in question. Later in her book, Mrs. Emmet described herself and Dr. von Baravalle as "perhaps the world's most complete optimists" (10), and she writes, "Leaving Edgewood and coming to the hill gave us the freedom to try to build a Waldorf School" (26). High Mowing opened with all four high school grades and 53 students, including five seniors who relocated from Greenwich to complete their education with Mrs. Emmet and her faculty. It was the first Waldorf high school in the United States, and remains the only boarding school in the United States that uses Waldorf methods. (Other high schools may have boarding programs, but they operate primarily as day schools.)

High Mowing based its curriculum on the Carnegie unit (120 hours of instruction per credit) and aimed to be college preparatory. This was "vitally necessary here in New England," according to Mrs. Emmet. "Surprisingly, we found there was time within the curriculum for creative work. This, of course, was necessary if we wished to lead our young into rounded human beings. With this curriculum we sent students to M.I.T., Harvard, Wellesley and so forth" (26).

Kimberton Farms School and The Waldorf School of Garden City

Baravalle left High Mowing after one year because of an unexplained family situation, and he spent the next several years as chair of the mathematics department at Adelphi College, now Adelphi University. While there, he met Alarik Myrin, a wealthy Swedish immigrant, retired from the Nobel brothers' oil business and married to Mabel Pew, a founder of what is now the Pew Charitable Trusts. "Those who knew him [Myrin]... share a vivid memory," according to Helen Wieneke, a former headmistress of the Kimberton School. "A tall, handsome man—curly-grey-haired, ruddy complexioned, impeccably groomed—standing beside his horse completely surrounded by children."

Myrin wished to establish a Waldorf school on his estate, a farm west of Philadelphia. Baravalle arranged for Elizabeth Grunelius, another teacher from the original school in Stuttgart, to move to Pennsylvania to assist in starting the Kimberton Farms School. She was joined by Virginia Birdsall, a teacher who had previously resigned from the

Steiner School in New York City. The new school, originally located in a house on Myrin's estate, had planned to open in October 1941 as a refuge for British children displaced by World War II. Although the school was provided, the children were never sent; most likely they were relocated within Britain. So, through word of mouth, the Myrins obtained twenty local children to attend the school.

Although Myrin was Swedish, like Baravalle he believed in the importance of Americanizing his Waldorf school:

> Mr. Myrin was adamant about selecting people from the area [of the Kimberton school]. He felt that they, as native plants, were a part of the local heritage and could establish a school with its own character. "The Waldorf method belongs to every country and every people, because it is universal,' he said repeatedly. "We are indebted to Rudolf Steiner for that method. It is our task to use it honestly and adapt it to Chester County, Pennsylvania." (Wieneke, 1970, 27)

The Myrin's estate was also the site of the Kimberton Farms Agricultural School for biodynamic farming, farming according to principles put forth by Rudolf Steiner, also founded in 1941. The agricultural school lasted only three years, but was visited frequently by Mr. Rodale, of *Organic Gardening* and Rodale Press (Gregg, 1970, 15).

The Kimberton Farms School was (in actuality) the fourth school founded in the United States that employed Rudolf Steiner's principles for the education of children, although it may claim to be the third; the High Mowing School presently does not acknowledge as part of its own history its early experiment in Connecticut. And, if we discount the Hale's little-known experiment in Maine, Kimberton can call itself the second Waldorf school in the United States.

Mr. Myrin, recognizing the importance for Waldorf schools of teachers familiar with Steiner's ideas, wanted to establish a teacher training institute or facility. His friend and educational expert Baravalle had just become chair of the mathematics department at Adelphi College, then a women's college. The college had been through bankruptcy proceedings and was financially strapped. Paul Dawson Eddy, president of the college, respected Dr. von Baravalle's teaching. He wrote:

After Dr. Baravalle began to teach at Adelphi, the number of mathematics majors increased sharply. I discovered by visiting his classes that his was a new and dynamic technique of teaching.... I was eager to learn more of the Waldorf method and the Steiner philosophy of education. He told me about the Kimberton Farms School... The Myrins invited Mrs. Eddy and me, along with Dr. Baravalle, to visit that school. Thus, one day in 1944, I met Alarik and Mabel Myrin for the first time. (1970)

That Baravalle did not direct Dr. Eddy to the Steiner School in New York City, hours closer than Kimberton, speaks again to his distancing himself from that school, but the reason or reasons remain unknown. It is equally clear, however, that Baravalle and Myrin had become closely allied, and Baravalle may have had good reasons for directing Eddy to Myrin.

As it was, the Myrins were later elected to Adelphi's board of trustees, at which point they assumed the balance of a large mortgage. In Eddy's words, "This was the break the college needed, and Mr. and Mrs. Myrin remained [Adelphi's] kind and understanding friends through the years" (39).

Eddy describes the founding of the Waldorf Demonstration School this way:

Mr. Myrin told me of a great hope of his. This was to train teachers in Waldorf School methods in an American college. He asked me whether Adelphi would be interested in such an undertaking. I assured him of my own interest, and he accepted my invitation to visit the college. There I suggested to him that Dr. Baravalle might teach a class in Waldorf methods as part of Adelphi's teacher education program, but added that it would be difficult to train teachers without a Waldorf demonstration school. Such a school, I thought, could begin with a nursery and kindergarten. Mr. Myrin decided that he would build this first unit and add more classrooms as they were needed. (1970)

The school opened in September 1947, and, by 1958, had started construction on a fifth expansion, its high school wing. It now occupies ten acres on the southwest corner of the Adelphi University campus. Across the street at that time was a square mile of fields, woods, and a stream, where children could play at recess; it is now a suburban development, part of Garden City South. Elizabeth de Grunelius left her position in Kimberton to teach in Garden City. A pamphlet she wrote on the design of a kindergarten playground is illustrated with drawings of the playgrounds she had built in Kimberton.

The Adelphi master's degree program in education included what we now call Waldorf teacher training. Unlike most such programs today, however, it insisted on a balance between conventional teacher training and training in Waldorf methods. It did not seek to separate "Waldorf" training from the training of teachers in general, but to incorporate Waldorf methods into general teacher training.

Quickly, however, the Garden City school, far from Mr. Myrin's daily gaze, discovered that Baravalle's personality was not entirely conducive to the expectations of American parents. It seems that Europeans, or at least Dr. von Baravalle, expected parents to send children to school and trust that their education was proceeding appropriately. American parents, or at least some of those in Garden City, were, or wanted to be, much more involved in their children's education. When they discovered Steiner's writings and discovered that Dr. von Baravalle was relatively loath to discuss them, the young school hit a shoal. It became important to find someone who could both guide the school and address the parents' questions. That man turned out to be John Gardner, who had left the Steiner School a dozen years earlier (Rose 1996).

John Gardner tells it this way:

...[F]rom the beginning [the Waldorf school] had been plagued by difficulties. Misunderstandings had arisen between its educational and administrative directors, and between its small nucleus of European Waldorf teachers and the several American teachers who were interested in the school project but had little grounding in the methods of Waldorf education. The conflicts were partly personal, partly matters of principle. Confusion and doubt had spread among the parents drawn to the new venture, and by the middle of the school's second year Mr. Myrin saw its very existence threatened. (1970, 41)

(Ironically, twenty-five years later, Mr. Gardner himself was to be the center of a crisis of confidence among parents at the school, one that involved two groups of the faculty, and that was partly personal, partly a matter of principle. More about this at the end of the chapter.)

The schism between the European faculty—Baravalle and Grunelius—and the Americans characterizes the birth of the new generation of Waldorf schools. It is also a schism that exists or echoes to this day. According to Uta Taylor-Weaver, who taught at the Stuttgart Waldorf School and also taught at the Garden City school, it has been and still is the case that European Waldorf teachers tend to see American teachers as superficial and American Waldorf teachers tend to see Europeans as dogmatic. Further, Taylor-Weaver believes that many among the first generation of Waldorf teachers, those who knew Steiner personally, especially, believe that they simply could not communicate all that they possessed regarding Waldorf education.

Because they found their audience unreceptive, in their opinion, the Europeans were not willing to share what they could have regarding esoteric points of Waldorf teaching. Specifically, Steiner's "Teachers' Meditations" were withheld by the first generation of teachers and only rediscovered and translated in the 1960s. These were then published, but distribution was restricted to numbered volumes available only to members of Waldorf school colleges of teachers. Finally, in the late 1990s, some of this material was retranslated and published as an appendix to Steiner's lectures called *Foundations of Human Experience*, available to anyone who wanted to read them. For such central concepts to be virtually lost and unavailable for almost a century speaks to the generational disputes and changes with which much of this book is concerned.

On the other hand, the younger generation believed strongly that it needed to work out teaching methods for itself, that a "principle of freedom," to quote Beulah Emmet, was more important than oral tradition or educational lineage (1991).

In 1949, according to Gardner, "Mr. Myrin... found it hard to realize that what was thoroughly congenial to him seemed to others dubious and foreign" (1970, 40). Myrin felt obliged to consult his trusted counselor, Franz E. Winkler, M.D., an anthroposophic doctor, author, and president of the Myrin Institute for Adult Education.

...Dr. Winkler remembered that I [Gardner] had taught in the Rudolf Steiner School in New York City for two years. He knew that I felt confined in my work as a Senior Supervisor of Adult Education for New York State... He suggested to Mr. Myrin that my dual acquaintance with Waldorf education and with public education might fit me to be of service at Adelphi. Perhaps if I replaced the administrative director of the demonstration school, I might find a way to heal the splits that had developed between... the European and American contingents in the school. (44-45)

Mr. Gardner accepted the job with the following conviction:

I thought [Waldorf education] belonged in the main stream of American culture and needed no excuses or shielding. There was nothing in Rudolf Steiner that Thoreau and Emerson and Whitman would not have approved wholeheartedly; indeed Steiner's deepest spiritual insights seemed to me more native, more congenial to many Americans than some of the merely cultural characteristics that Waldorf education had brought with it from Europe. (46)

Mr. Gardner's American convictions may represent an extreme— High Mowing had a much more international faculty and seemed not to suffer the same schism, and Kimberton seems to have developed more slowly.

Other evidence of the American convictions of the Garden City school may be found in the "outreach" activities with which it was associated. Mr. Myrin also founded the Myrin Institute for Adult Education, based on an anthroposophic understanding of the world. The first president of the Institute was Dr. Winkler. The Institute sought to further an intuitive understanding of the world, similar to that sought by Waldorf schools, by sponsoring conferences and publishing proceedings by anthroposophists and "fellow travelers" of note, including, for example, authors Laurens van der Post and R. D. Lawrence; and educators Patricia Brown and Jeffrey Kane. In addition, Gardner was a founding member of the Council for Educational Freedom in America, Inc., in Washington, D.C., which sought separation of school and state, well ahead of recent concerns over school choice, charters, and vouchers. (See, for example, Gardner, 1976.)

Some Waldorf schools today may see themselves as "against" a dominant "McCulture," but the Garden City school, at least in its first decades, actively sought to promote a conversation about change, not to withdraw and criticize. This activity, in my mind, speaks to the confidence with which Gardner and others could address questions of the place of Waldorf education in society. Al Tomlinson (1999), who taught in Garden City for more than forty years, remembers, "[Gardener] sure knew a lot about Steiner. He would answer all questions from all quarters and answer them sensibly, so he didn't scare people off." The Garden City School grew quickly under Gardner's leadership, graduating its first high school class in 1960, and constructing wings to hold a student body of more than three hundred by 1973.

A Crisis

In 1973 or 1974, following the death of Franz Winkler a year or two earlier (George Rose [1996] described Dr. Winkler as "an anchor for Mr. Gardner"), John Gardner apparently became convinced that one of his former students, a young man named Richard Walton, was clairvoyant. In a word not often used then, Walton could allegedly "channel" spiritual beings, including, some claimed, Jesus Christ and the Hebrew patriarch Abraham. Through these voices or beings, or through a correlated power of insight, Walton gradually became, allegedly, a spiritual advisor to Gardner and other members of the Waldorf School community.

Gardner retired as faculty chair in 1975 and was connected to the Waldorf School of Garden City only through his teacher training program at Adelphi University, his office at the south end of the Waldorf School building, and the considerable respect he was accorded by the institution. He gradually introduced Walton to sympathetic members of the school community, including several teachers at the school. Others, however, saw no good in Walton's proposed spiritual leadership. By 1978, parents and some members of the faculty at the school got wind of Mr. Gardner's allegiance and began to question his judgment. When a mundane faculty decision—whether or not to allow a student to drop a foreign language class, by one account (Rose 1996)—was made in consultation with Walton, several parents demanded that the school investigate its relationship to Gardner and to Walton.

The faculty invited Gardner and Walton to their weekly faculty meeting. Walton demonstrated his clairvoyance (Rose 1996, Tomlinson 1999). Those who already supported Walton continued to do so, but many who had not supported him saw only danger and even evil in the course his influence represented (Rose 1996). Remarkably, no one with whom I spoke who was present at this meeting suggested that Walton was a charlatan or that he was insincere, at least with regard to his apparent ability. The question for many at the school was whether or not Walton's apparent ability arose from true spiritual insight or from some other, presumably destructive, spiritual force.

Peter Curran, a respected history teacher in Garden City, had managed to avoid the turmoil at the school because he spent much of the academic year at Camp Glen Brook in Marlborough, New Hampshire, the Waldorf School's rural campus. The faculty invited him to mediate the dispute between those who supported Gardner and Walton and those who opposed their influence. According to more than one account, Curran heard days of discussion, requested resignations from the entire faculty, and accepted three, including that of the faculty chair (Curran 1990, Rose 1996). Gardner was not then employed by the school, but Adelphi University heard enough of the scandal to cancel the program that Mr. Gardner headed.

In the aftermath, many families left the school, some in sympathy with Gardner, others simply because the whole event was so outlandish. Similarly, many members of the faculty resigned, in sympathy with Gardner, in disgust at the way in which the conflict was resolved, or again, because of an unwillingness to engage with such peculiarities.

At least one teacher, Lawrence Williams, later wrote about these events:

In 1979 ... the real force behind the school was John Gardner, who had been Faculty Chairman of the school for about twenty years. During that time he had developed a solid reputation as an extraordinary human being of almost mythic proportions. Tall and robust, with pure white hair, he radiated strength and wisdom wherever he went, and he guided the school and presided over the teacher meetings with a firm hand and a warm heart.

As soon as I started teaching there, I felt I had come home. During his career as Faculty Chairman of the school, Dr. [sic] Gardner had developed it into a full K-12 school and assembled a group of remarkable teachers. Strong, experienced and supportive, these teachers provided the guidance I needed, and with their help I was daily realizing more of my own potential as a teacher. Every Wednesday we had a faculty meeting, and this meeting provided inspiration and support for all of us, and served to meld us together into a cohesive unit.

…what I didn't know was that all I was experiencing was about to change. Underneath this idyllic scene, a storm was brewing that would transform this extraordinary school into a maelstrom of bitterness and conflict and dramatically change the life of every teacher there.

The story of the collapse of the Garden City Waldorf School is very complex, and it would take an entire book to explore all the intricacies of it and attempt to understand what really happened. Since this isn't my main concern at this time, I'll simply say that—from my perspective—it was a classic case of a battle between life and form played out in the context of very strong personalities.

…In his twenty years as Faculty Chairman, John Gardner had carefully crafted a strong, clear form based upon the pedagogical teachings of Rudolf Steiner, but in recent years … Gardner had begun to feel the limitations of the form he had created and felt that the teachers needed to be guided more by the spirit instead of the outer forms, so he had started encouraging some of the teachers to use their own spiritual perceptions in their educational approach, rather than automatically adhering to the traditional form. As word of this began to spread throughout the school, more of the teachers became interested in following this approach, especially many of the younger teachers. However, even though the initial results of this approach did not conflict with Steiner's guiding principles for Waldorf schools, it set off a firestorm between those teachers who felt we should follow the traditional forms that had made the school what it was, and those who wanted to explore new approaches guided by the spirit.

As November passed into December, the teachers became more and more polarized, and the weekly teacher meetings that used to provide such inspiration and support soon became battlegrounds for the warring factions. As the tension in the school escalated, the parents of the students in the school became angry and demanded a resolution. When a resolution was not immediately forthcoming, the parents began to boycott the school by taking their children out and refusing to make their monthly tuition payments. Soon, the situation became desperate. If a resolution wasn't reached within a week, the school would have to close. The teachers called in an outside arbitrator, Peter Curran, who had been associated with the school for many years but who was not currently teaching at the school.

Mr. Curran met with all of the teachers as a group and listened to all of us present our views of the situation. After several hours of listening, he stopped the discussion and said he had two final questions to ask.

"Do you want the school to continue?"

This took us by surprise, because we had never really asked ourselves that question. We had all assumed that the school would continue, so we were only arguing about what the guiding principles of the school should be. But now it was clear that the school was in real danger of closing within a few days unless the situation was resolved. As we discussed the possibility of closing the school, we all agreed that if we were to do that—even for the most noble of educational principles—the ones who would be hurt the most would be the children. Whatever our philosophical disagreements might have been, we were united by a love for the children in the school, and we couldn't stand to hurt them any more than they had already been hurt. We voted unanimously, "Yes," we wanted the school to continue.

"Are you willing to accept and abide by whatever decisions I must make in order to keep the school alive?"

We all swallowed hard as we considered the implications of this, but we knew that the situation had progressed to a point that someone had to make the hard decisions necessary to keep the school alive, and quarreling over those decisions would only paralyze us further and force the school to close. The time for discussion was past; it was time for action. Again we voted unanimously, "Yes," we would abide by his decisions.

"Thank you," he said. "That's all I need to know." The meeting was adjourned.

The next day, we learned that everyone strongly aligned with the "spirit-led" group had either been fired or resigned, and older teachers who were experienced in the traditional approaches had been hired to replace them. In the end, it was simply a matter of finances. As a very pragmatic New Englander, Peter Curran had cut through the philosophical debates and seen the obvious truth. On a purely practical level, the only thing that keeps a school alive is the tuition paid by the parents, so if the school was to continue, he had to find out what the parents wanted and move in that direction. The majority of the parents supported the traditionalists, so the choice was clear: everyone associated with the new impulse had to leave.

It was a clean sweep. About a dozen teachers were fired [sic], Andy Leaf resigned as Faculty Chairman of the school, Dr. Gardner resigned as Director of the Waldorf Institute, the Institute was to be closed at the end of the school year, and Peter Curran assumed the position of temporary Faculty Chairman until a permanent Chairman could be elected by the teachers. (1997)

It is curious that Williams neglects to mention Walton, the center of the whirlpool of the events he narrates. And the parent unrest that Williams mentions centered around the relationship of Gardner and others to Walton, not to teachers being "guided more by the spirit." Long Island *Newsday* and the New York *Times* both covered the story. Here is the *Times* version:

"Psychic" Ex-Student's Influence Shakes Waldorf School
by John T. McQuiston
Special to The New York Times

GARDEN CITY, L.I., Feb. 16 [1979] — The Waldorf School, founded here 32 year ago on the philosophy that a teacher must nurture the intuitive and spiritual nature of students as well as their physical and intellectual needs, has been deeply split by charges that some staff members, including the former headmaster, came under the psychic influence of a former student.

The resignations of the headmaster, the high school principal, the librarian and four teachers—and the withdrawal of scores of students—have left the private school's immediate future in doubt. And next week, Adelphi University will decide whether to continue the student-teacher training program it has operated in affiliation with the school.

Marvin A. Iverson, the dean of graduate arts and sciences at Adelphi, said today that the university's affiliation with Waldorf would be formally reviewed at a meeting of the Graduate Academic Affairs Committee on Tuesday, and that there was "no anticipation of continuing the program with Waldorf."

The Center of the Dispute

The program involves the training of 20 student teachers a year, who then sought teaching positions within the loosely affiliated network of about 80 Waldorf schools in the United States and Europe.

One of these student teachers, 25-year-old Richard Walton, who was a former student at Waldorf, is at the center of the dispute that has divided the faculty, students and parents at the preparatory school in this relatively prosperous, conservative residential community 25 miles east of Manhattan.

What was described as "internal chaos" began when Mr. Walton, who has said that he is able to communicate with "certain beings in the spiritual world," allegedly used these "powers" to advise school officials on matters ranging from language curriculum to what music to play at a school dance.

As his influence reportedly grew among leading faculty members and with John F. Gardner, a former headmaster and, at the time, director of the Waldorf Institute, other staff and faculty members became resentful, called a meeting and voted to seek the resignations of those who accepted his suggestions.

Departure Deplored

As a result, Peter MacNair the high school principal, Edward Blatchford, a teacher and ninth-grade advisor, and John Bickart, a teacher and 10th grade advisor, resigned, followed by several others, including Carroll Scherer, the librarian, Andrew Leaf, the headmaster, and Mr. Gardner.

Mr. Gardner's departure from the Waldorf Institute was regarded as "very serious" by Dean Iverson of Adelphi. "With his resignation," said the dean, there is "no one of his stature at Waldorf to continue the teacher-training program."

Joanne Pisano, a co-chairman of the school's parent group, said tonight that she doubted the end of the long affiliation between Waldorf and Adelphi "would have any serious effect on the Waldorf system."

She said she preferred not to comment on the change of administration at Waldorf, saying only that "things are going well now."

The school's new headmaster, Peter A. Curran, a former history teacher at the school, was away on vacation and could not be reached to comment on next Tuesday's meeting at Adelphi. Classes are to resume at Waldorf on Tuesday. The school was closed this week for a mid-winter holiday.

I have little doubt that the turmoil and the tension between the school's ideals and the destructive events of this time contributed, years later, to my decision to research and write about the history of Waldorf schools. I last saw Mr. Gardner in the spring of 1997. I hoped to record his version of the events narrated above. He agreed to an interview to be conducted in the fall of 1997, but passed away in July.

In the larger story of Waldorf education in the United States, it strikes me particularly that Gardner was displaced by his seeming inability to reconcile his allegiance to Walton with his allegiance to, especially, the parents at the school. Both Walton and the parents were members of a generation younger than Gardner, who himself had entered in 1949 by displacing the chief representative of the Europeans, Baravalle, who in his turn had been ousted for his inability to hear the parents of his own day. Gardner's adherence to what he clearly saw as a principle of truth and value nearly destroyed the school to which he had dedicated much of his life. An apparent inability to bridge generations (not that there weren't also more personal and more important issues for many involved) exacerbated the school's difficulties.

An American Form?

At least two people with whom I spoke disputed or minimized my suggestion of generational change from a European to an American influence. The first was John Brousseau, of the Highland Hall School in Los Angeles. In response to a question about conversations regarding an American form of Waldorf education, different from an earlier German import, he said:

> The individuals obviously had their personal quirks and European biases and all, but the education somehow stayed free of that as far as my experience was concerned.... I was surprised to find myself in independent education. That was more surprising than the issue of American or European, which wasn't really one at all. (1999)

Brousseau did not become a teacher until the mid-1960s, however, by which point the generational changes I describe had largely been accomplished.

Lucy Schneider, teacher and then faculty chair at the Steiner School in New York, in response to a question about translating Waldorf education for an American clientele, replied:

> I think actually that has colored the school from day one. It's very interesting being the first school [in the United States] and yet it was less influenced by European teachers than some of the other schools. For example, in Toronto, the distinct flavor of Alan Howard and of England live so strongly.... Our school was formed by Americans who went to Europe. But they went to Europe ... to explore. They were wide open young people like the MacKaye family, true artists, and I sometimes get the feeling that they really weren't sure what they were teaching. And it really didn't matter because they would just get in front of these students and give them such richness and so many gifts.... I think there has always been this

feisty and artistic root in our school, which affected it and didn't create a very European influence despite the fact that we had many teachers who came from Europe who were very strong, such as William Harrer, Rudolf Koppel, and Ruth Pusch.... They wrote letters to Dornach [Switzerland; the seat of the leadership of the Anthroposophical Society] in the early years telling them how they were doing. (1999)

I don't dispute Schneider's remarks; I believe they support some of my claims about the Europeans. (I have deliberately restricted my research to the United States, and cannot comment on the Toronto school.) But in comparison to the deliberate agendas of Myrin and Gardner at Kimberton and Garden City, I believe we can say that a balance was tipped from modest questions of American identity to a quest to forge something new, different, and appropriate to the North American continent.

This quest necessarily raised a particularly American question: what is the relationship of Waldorf schools to African Americans? Because all Waldorf schools of this generation were relatively exclusive independent schools, the question was not as visibly urgent as it might otherwise have been. Faculty meeting minutes from the Rudolf Steiner School in New York record a first application by a black student on October 11, 1944. The ensuing discussion is illustrative of the contest between imperfect teachers and an ideal they know they should hold. One states firmly that "there is no question of accepting the boy if he's qualified," while another wonders if the school isn't being singled out as a "test case." The faculty decides to pass the matter before the board of trustees before making a final decision, recognizing the potential economic consequences. Unfortunately, future minutes do not record whether or not the applicant was admitted.

Of equal importance to the question of the admission of the black applicant was a corollary discussion on the same day in which it was recorded that the school had an "unwritten rule" that no class would be constituted of more than one-fourth Jewish children. The minutes make clear that this rule was not referred to when a particular trustee, who was Jewish, was present. Further research may establish whether or not this policy was ever enforced, although its very existence argues that the question was raised at least once. Given the influx of Jewish refugees before and during WWII, and given the Steiner School's particular and contested interpretation of itself as a "Christian" school, we can comprehend the perceived cultural threat while deploring the policy.

In all, the discussion in the minutes, despite a suspicious teacher or two, strikes a contemporary reader as relatively enlightened, coming as it did in the year of Gunnar Myrdal's *An American Dilemma* (1944/1996), a discussion of "the Negro problem" in the United States and almost a decade before the Civil Rights movement really started to move. In the case of this discussion, it may be said, Steiner's ideas provide a scaffold useful for promoting an anti-racist act: the potential admission of a black student. And when a racist policy—a quota on Jews—is discussed, it is not justified with recourse to Steiner's ideas. In 1944, among one small American school faculty, it is clear that Steiner is considered an anti-racist.

We could say that the question was dealt with reactively by the Americans, admitting black applicants as they appeared in ones and twos, but not altering admissions procedures or curriculum to accommodate cultural or social differences. The question was dealt with more proactively by the next generation, the Alternatives, in adding African tales, geography, and history to their curricula. Finally, in the last couple of decades, the nation has seen a truly public, predominantly African-American Waldorf school in the choice system of the Milwaukee public schools (see next chapter). Compared with the proportion of African Americans in the United States, however, consideration from Waldorf schools has been minimal. I believe there are two reasons for this. The first is economic: although more than ten percent of children in the United States attend non-public schools, relatively few of these children are African American. Second, attempts to "Americanize" Waldorf school curricula—by including the Transcendentalists, for example—were not initially made with African American experience in mind. Further, in general, the more progressive, child-centered perception of Waldorf schools may not appeal to African-Americans who have, with good reason, often sought more rigorous, traditional forms of education.

Evolution

It is not a focus of my research to compare Waldorf schools with other independent or parochial schools, but it does occur to me (perhaps out of ignorance) that my generational interpretation of the growth of Waldorf school in the United States does not apply, or applies in a smaller degree, to these other schools. Waldorf schools strike a balance, I would argue, between schools that are given a mission or impetus at their founding and then find their way forward, changing as conditions change, but hewing closely to their originally perceived task; and schools that sprout up following each tidal shift or pendulum swing in educational theory and practice. The first set of schools might be established independent schools on Michael Katz's "corporate volunteer" model (1989). A relatively conservative board of trustees ensures that change is slow.

The second set of schools might include, presently, charter schools and for-profit schools that have sprung up in immediate response to a perceived problem with education as it is.

Waldorf schools have a general mission (however hard it may be to express succinctly), and this mission includes an evolutionary sense of their own existence; a sense that I believe to be relatively unique. Because of this balance between continuity and change in Waldorf schools (what Oberman terms "form and flexibility" and I call "promise and compromise"), the history of Waldorf schools may be indexed with social and cultural change in the United States. The transition from the Europeans to the Americans occurred during and immediately after the Second World War, a time when a U.S. identity and ethos grew rapidly. And the change from the Americans to the Alternatives similarly mirrors changes in the 1960s and 1970s from a more consensus-driven to a more conflict-driven notion of American identity.

3. THE ALTERNATIVES

I CALL THE THIRD GENERATION OF WALDORF SCHOOLS The Alternatives. Waldorf schools seek to make their positions secure as alternatives to what they see as more conventional schooling, even if that schooling is older-style Waldorf schooling. This generation consists of at least 150 schools. The number of Waldorf schools in the United States more or less doubled every ten years between 1928 and the end of the twentieth century, so the first generation consists of one school only; the second of between eight and sixteen; and this third of most of the rest between, say, 1965 and the present. A fourth generation, the Social Missionaries, beginning in the early 1990s, consists of a few dozen more schools.

We may look back and see older schools as constituting part of "alternative education," but these schools did not see themselves this way. The Waldorf School of Garden City was founded as a "demonstration" school with the clear aim of proving the validity of Steiner's methods for education in general. Waldorf schools that were founded in the mid-1960s and later saw themselves not at the forefront of educational change, however; not as experiments, but as alternatives. At first these may be labeled "countercultural," later "new age," but this aspect of their existence is a tangent to my topic.

Initially, I parsed the generations differently, separating "the counterculture" from "the new age." I came to believe, however, that continuity here is stronger than any distinction I cared to draw. The so-called new age is an extension of the counterculture. It is in some ways the mature counterculture, now become tame, acceptable, middle-class, commercialized (with its own press and products). It is no longer "counter," but now "alternative," and, perhaps, more effective; in regard particularly, for example, to such issues as awareness of human desecration of the environment.

The Sacramento Waldorf School

I choose the Sacramento Waldorf School as the first school in this generation. It existed as a tenuous initiative between 1959 and 1965, but gained strength and vision—as a school of the new generation—with the arrival of Betty Staley and a small cohort from Kimberton, Pennsylvania. (For an excellent account of the Sacramento school before 1965, see Oberman, 1999.) In leaving Pennsylvania and the older, established, more authoritarian structure of Kimberton, and in choosing to migrate to Sacramento, Staley and friends symbolize the change from one generation to the next. They renounced one way of doing things and chose an alternative.

Here is Betty Staley:

Franklin Kane, then my husband, interviewed at [the] Kimberton [Farm School, PA] with Mrs. Myrin [wife of Alarik Myrin, founder of the school]. We moved to Kimberton in late August [1961]. A group of teachers at Kimberton really wanted it to become a Waldorf school. It considered itself a Waldorf School, but it had a headmistress. Mrs. Weinecke, the former headmistress, had retired. Mrs. Lord was the headmistress. She was very strong and wasn't about to give up power to a college of teachers. Also, several of the teachers were public school teachers; Mrs. Myrin wanted that. And Franklin would come home frustrated at the decisions that were made, especially, for example, regarding a heavy public school reading program and tests that were given in the early grades. Kimberton then was a Main Line sort of prep school. Franklin and the others were more and more frustrated. Because of our dissatisfaction, we were singled out as a group of troublemakers. (1999)

For Staley, a true Waldorf school could not have a head of school, but should be run by a "college of teachers" who "work out of anthroposophy." The school should follow methods that oppose unnecessary testing or too-early reading. These understandings are common among Waldorf teachers today, but cannot necessarily be located in Steiner's work; and they clearly were not in the understanding of some earlier anthroposophists like Alarik Myrin and Hermann von Baravalle. They were willing to compromise; Staley, at that time, was not. She continues:

In our fourth year we decided that it was now or never; something had to happen. René Querido came to give some lectures. We'd known René from our training so we went to talk to him. He said he'd see what he could do. Several meetings were held of all those who were interested in the school really becoming an anthroposophical school. René facilitated the meetings. It became clear that the group was not willing to buck Mrs. Myrin. One said she owed too much to Mrs. Myrin. Another said we should be patient; it wouldn't be long until Mrs. Myrin died and then we would become a Waldorf school. He wasn't about to stand up to her. But we could not live in a situation in which we were hoping for someone to die. René did not try to get us to leave but he helped us to clarify the situation. He got blamed for our leaving for years, but it wasn't his fault.

We gathered on Saturday night on Thanksgiving weekend to find out where we were each going to go. We had decided to leave Kimberton, but we had no plans to go anywhere together.

Now, I had written a letter to Stewart Easton [author of *Man and World in the Light of Anthroposophy* and a history professor at City College of New York] asking him if he would be godfather to my son. He hadn't answered for three months, but the Monday after our Saturday meeting a letter from him arrived saying that he had been in Sacramento. He had advised the Waldorf school there to close unless it could find five trained American Waldorf teachers. Well, five of us had met on Saturday night. I called him right away and said we were all leaving Kimberton. He asked us not to; he was friendly with people there. But he gave me the names and numbers to call in Sacramento and he sent us his thick report on the Sacramento school.

The five of us arranged to fly out there on New Year's Eve weekend. The school was a little bundle of shacks; it was filthy. We met with the board and two teachers. There were only two or three teachers left; the others had all been fired or were leaving. One was out with a nervous breakdown. We learned about the financial situation, which was awful, and we learned about the history of the school. We thought Sacramento was an impossible place to live. But we all decided to move, regardless. The board accepted our conditions, and we ran the school by telephone from Pennsylvania for the rest of the year. Our group of five made every decision. (Staley 1999)

A Symbol of the Change

This group's idea that a school should be run by the faculty (even if the "faculty" had yet to teach a child at the school, had yet to move to California to occupy the school) is perhaps the greatest symbol of the generation I am calling the Alternatives. In her own evolution as a teacher and administrator, however, Staley herself has learned that this notion was "of her time" and did not necessarily represent a truth about Waldorf schools or Rudolf Steiner's prescription for them. As she acknowledges in her introduction to *Faculty Meetings with Rudolf Steiner*, "It has often been said that Waldorf schools are 'faculty run.' The translation of the term *Selbstverwaltung*, however, is much closer to 'self-administered.' There are many misunderstandings around this issue…" (1998, xxiii). She goes on to note that Steiner himself was director of the first Waldorf School from its founding until his death, and his responsibilities included hiring and firing teachers.

Uta Taylor-Weaver (undated) attributes the direction of Waldorf schools in England and the United States by a relatively small and exclusive "College of Teachers" to Anglophone mistranslations of concepts like the German *Collegium*. What in Germany would be a group of colleagues becomes, in translation, an exclusive membership. Staley's reexamination of the concept of self-administration in Waldorf schools contributes to characteristics of a fourth generation of Waldorf schools in the United States.

Steiner himself, in another context, said:

I can well imagine, for example, that there are national societies who will most certainly want to employ democratic procedures. I

can also imagine that there will be others who will want to be thoroughly aristocratic in their approach… In a general way, however, I
do not find this question to be of paramount importance as a matter
of principle. …[In] practice, there will be little difference between
democracy and aristocracy. …Anyone who is expected to carry
out a function [whether elected or appointed] must have freedom
above all else. …Whether democracy or aristocracy is the method,
the society will not look much different. (Steiner, 1990a, 89-91)

Steiner is speaking here of the founding of national societies within
the larger Anthroposophical Society, but he may as well be describing
the organization and administration of schools. Both the Society and
any schools are cultural institutions. They must represent the communities in which they exist, and they must select members to accomplish
particular tasks. For Steiner, clearly, the point is not the method but the
outcome—based on knowledge and accompanied by freedom.

Another Generational Distinction

Staley's story of the founding of the Sacramento school continues:

Betty Buck, part of an early Californian anthroposophic study
group, started the Sacramento school. A small group including
Betty invited [Hermann von] Baravalle to come from Los Angeles
to lecture in Sacramento. Two people came. And Baravalle said—he
told me this directly later—that if there's only one person there,
you give your presentation as if there were thousands. He gave
his lecture, and those two people went on to start the Sacramento
Waldorf School. It began in the home of a well-known health food
storeowner, Mr. Elliott, in Sacramento, and it began with two children. By the end of the year I believe it had 40 children, and then
it grew and grew. (1999)

Alarik Myrin was an international industrialist; Mr. Elliott ran a
health food store. Here lies another image of the distinction between
earlier Waldorf schools and later ones, between the Americans and the
Alternatives. Staley continues:

The early teachers didn't know very much about Waldorf education. Baravalle—this became very serious—did not mention the Anthroposophical Society. He trained the teachers initially, but in method only. He—and Mr. Myrin—"cleaned up" Steiner's lectures, removing spiritual or esoteric references to anthroposophy. He believed Americans would be put off by it. (2003)

According to Al Tomlinson, a student of Baravalle at Adelphi College in the 1940s and later a long-time teacher at the Waldorf School of Garden City, Baravalle believed that Americans were more practically-minded than were Germans or Europeans in general. He made it a practice to avoid Steiner's esotericism in presenting Waldorf education to Americans (Tomlinson 1999). As Oberman points out, Baravalle was one of few lecturers whom Steiner himself approved to speak for anthroposophy (1999). Although Staley and others of the Alternative generation find little value in Baravalle's approach—find it often duplicitous—it clearly had value in that Baravalle was associated with the founding of nearly every Waldorf school in the United States from the 1930s to the 1960s. He has been called the "Johnny Appleseed" of Waldorf education in the United States. Staley herself draws a distinction between old ways and new:

We were absolutely certain when we moved to Sacramento that we would not have another Kimberton. We would not have the strict form. We learned year by year, of course, that you need form. Eventually we acknowledged that Kimberton had had something to offer, but at first we were very much against what we had experienced there. For example, we chose to live away from each other so there wouldn't be the kind of judgments that we experienced at Kimberton. At Kimberton, others would notice and comment if your light was on late at night, or your television. It was awful. It didn't come so much from Mrs. Myrin, but from a kind of anthroposophical inbreeding. On the other hand, Mrs. Myrin was like a lady of the castle. Once she stopped her chauffeur to say—I was outside hanging up laundry—that would be perfectly all right if I wanted to cut lilacs from the bushes in front of our house. Or at Christmas we would get these beautiful fruit baskets, and Mrs.

Myrin's assistant would have called and gotten the sizes of all of our children's clothes and there would be beautiful clothes from Lord & Taylor—which we would return to buy less expensive clothing. We felt like peons, Franklin more than I.

So we went to Sacramento to be a non-Kimberton school and to be a real Waldorf School. We arrived at a difficult time. A German teacher had just been fired for hitting a kid. Another teacher was still absent due to a breakdown. A parent or two, untrained, were teaching. And the school had gotten the reputation of being a Nazi school because there were Germans there and one of them had hit a child.

And there had been a terrible split. The teachers who had been trained by Baravalle were taught certain ways to do things, and they never knew there was an Anthroposophical Society or books by Steiner that they could buy. They got everything from Baravalle. The teachers from Germany—I believe they had come to Los Angeles, but there were no jobs and they heard that Sacramento was desperate for teachers—spoke about the Society and anthroposophy, and they also had very German ways of doing things. There was a terrible clash, with each side judging the other. Meanwhile these German teachers didn't know how to handle a class without hitting the children. This was all before we came. It was a bloodletting.

So the first year was rough. The enrollment had dropped to 60 through sixth grade. The school had gone through eighth grade, but had to drop back. The school was really suffering. Franklin and other teachers would give talks—you know, library talks, Rotary talks, anything. They were exhausted by it but they had to try and turn this thing around. They kept working and began to get a little bit of the enrollment back. It helped that most of them were American. Things started to stabilize during that year.

I stepped in when the kindergarten teacher was sick, and I taught kindergarten for a couple of months. Then we needed a craft teacher. I'd always loved crafts and so I said, okay, that I'll do. It was part time and I could bring the baby and bring the children, so I began teaching crafts in the school. Gradually the reputation of the school got better. Some of the teachers who had left came back and that strengthened the school, and it began to really grow.

We fought. We faced a crisis among the new faculty members; who was more anthroposophic than the other?

One teacher [I'll call him B], who had come from Highland Hall [in Los Angeles], was very charismatic and had almost a hypnotic effect. He had visions and he could see things. Franklin and other teachers were seen as being too pragmatic, and B and a few followers saw themselves as true believers. Decisions would come out of B's visions, and this started to split the faculty and parents. It was trouble.

We had founded a college of teachers a year or two before this, with the help of Francis Edmunds [an English anthroposophist, teacher, and friend to many American Waldorf schools], and the college was being torn to pieces. The charismatic group wanted to start a new college. They didn't have confidence in the college, even though they were in it, because they didn't have confidence in the other people. They wanted to have a new college for those who were "spiritually advanced." One teacher was so fanatic he wouldn't have fluorescent lights in his room, so he tore them out. There were no other lights and so he had the kids bring lamps into the classroom. B decided our new classrooms should be geodesic domes.

Francis [Edmunds] had just left after a visit—he came every February—he had just left us to go down to LA. We called him, and he turned around and flew right back up. It was extremely important. He sat with us as we identified the issues. We went around and asked, "Who's going to be here Monday morning?" We fired the one who had pulled the lights out; he's the one who had the breakdown earlier. I took his class at 1:00 in the morning. He was the only one who said he wouldn't continue working with the whole group. He was told that if he stirred up the parents he wouldn't get paid for the rest of the year, but he did stir up the parents. This had been his third time hired back into the school; we were naive. We gave him another chance after he had been fired and that was a mistake. So I became a class teacher Monday morning at 1:00. The rebel group was told that they were to shape up or ship out.

This group still believed they were right, however, and still believed they could change the school. It was difficult. The "visionary" man was doing all kinds of manipulations with the kids, mind things. Like he would say, "There's a number on the door, can anyone see the number?" He would encourage a bizarre kind of visioning. The parents were just screaming about him.

We needed to move, the school had outgrown itself, and we found a piece of land that is now the home of the school. When we moved, we took B out of the classroom and put him in charge of the buildings. But that didn't work out, either, and, in the end, we had to fire him. The geodesic domes, moved from our previous location, leaked. He bought a thousand desks as surplus, but they just rotted away in storage. He couldn't handle the buildings.

"Alternative" did not mean "experimental" in the sense that word attained in the 1960s, nor did it especially mean "politically liberal." Teachers saw their mission clearly in terms of meaning and human values. The issue for Staley was not form in Kimberton and formlessness in California; it was an older form discarded in favor of a newer:

Sacramento did not have the flower child mentality or drugs when we went there in 1965, obviously. It has been a very conservative school. We heard rumors many times that Highland Hall was a school of heart or freedom and Sacramento was a school of head or form. And we did create form, there's no question. The school faculty was never involved in the peace movement; that came in with the younger generation. The teachers, you know, they're half a generation too old. It's always been frustrating to me that the school has been so conservative and unwilling to take risks. (1999)

The Quality of Countercultural Consciousness

I did not have access to faculty meeting minutes or other primary documents for this generation, nor did I have primary experience of such a school (as I did in Garden City). The story of this generation is informed, therefore, by brief oral histories like Staley's quoted above. Those interviewed come universally from a well-educated, reflective group. Our interviews were convivial, open, and frank. Nonetheless, memory is demonstrably unreliable. To that end I have tried to correlate dates mentioned with events like school foundings, for example. Finally, the Alternatives take at face value the effectiveness or worth of Steiner's methods; where a generation earlier they needed to be demonstrated in experimental schools, they are now virtually self-evident. To the new generation, founding schools is good medicine. Society ails, and one way to address a myriad of social ills is to educate children according to Steiner's principles.

A Different Experience

Interviews with people who came of age in the 1960s, who taught in, or who helped to found schools between 1965 and 1990, demonstrate a quality of experience significantly different from that of the Europeans or the Americans. Within a conversation about alternatives, they demonstrate a new openness to spiritual seeking, practice, and conversation.

John Brousseau, teacher at the Highland Hall Waldorf School in Los Angeles:

My first encounter with Waldorf education was a bulletin board at an esoteric seminar that I attended. It was inviting people to a holiday fair. My wife and I went and were met by this most interesting elderly woman who greeted us as though she had known us a long time.

Barbara Shell, among the founders of and a teacher at the Emerson Waldorf School in North Carolina:

I decided to get an astrological chart done. I asked around for the best astrologer in the town in which I was living, and several people I respected all gave me the name of the same man. So I went to him, and he did my chart, and after looking at my chart, he went to his bookshelf and picked out a book by Rudolf Steiner and handed it to me. This was in 1976. He said, "I think you need to read this book." (1999)

Grace Sanders, among the founders of and a former admissions director at the Pasadena Waldorf School:

My sister was studying education and she had her children in the Sacramento Waldorf School.... She wrote a paper on Eckincar and Scientology and Rudolf Steiner's form of education.... We finally went to visit the [Sacramento] school after eight years. We walked into the garden, my husband Barry [Sanders, author of *A is for Ox*; retired professor at Pitzer College] and I, and something was just emanating from the ground, I have to say. It was truly a mystical moment. We looked around and sat there for about five minutes, then we walked into the bookstore. I picked up a bunch of books and then we drove home for eight hours. This was in the early '70s, by the way. I read aloud from these books for eight hours, so my throat was hoarse, and I remember pulling into our driveway in Claremont. My husband just turned to me and said, "Well, we have to find a Waldorf school." (1999)

Joan Almon, longtime kindergarten teacher and head of the Waldorf Early Childhood Alliance of North America:

In 1971 in Baltimore I was part of a community of people that was looking for new ideas for spiritual impulses in education. It was a community of about 12 people. Just before I moved in, the community had decided to start a kindergarten with the idea that everyone had a spark of spirit within them, and there had to be a way to keep it alive. We all felt we were struggling to bring this spark back to life, and we were convinced there was a way to educate children that would keep it alive. So I moved in, I heard about this plan, and it interested me. But I lacked the courage to say, "I'll do it." It took me several months, but finally, because they were looking for one more person to work in the kindergarten, I said that I would do it. We opened in October of 1971. We had some very good ideas and some very strange ideas. And none of us were very experienced with young children. The other two were teachers but of elementary age and now suddenly we were working with 4 and 5 year olds.

We were sort of neo-hippies—this was 1971 so it was just past the hippie era. One of the people had come out of the free school movement, one had come out of the public school movement. I had lived in San Francisco for a couple of years but on the fringe of the hippie movement. The community itself was not hippie-ish in that we were not into drugs, not into alcohol. We were a community that had learned its lesson about premarital sex and how destructive that can be, so it was basically a celibate community except for married couples. We didn't fit the model of a hippie community.

It was spiritually-oriented community without any single spiritual teaching. Everybody was very free to find their own. Most people were western-oriented rather than eastern-oriented, so we were exploring western esotericism but had never heard of Rudolf Steiner in the beginning. However there was a lot of interest in the Theosophical Society which existed in Baltimore, but there was no Anthroposophy in Baltimore at that point. So after a few months one of the teachers went to an education conference over Christmas down in Virginia Beach.

She met Werner Glas there. [Glas was an anthroposophist, professor at Mercy College, Detroit, and founder of a teacher training institute in Detroit that later moved to Spring Valley, New York, as Sunbridge College.] And after she heard him talk about Waldorf she asked if she could talk to him and describe what we were trying to do.

He said, "If that's what you're trying to do, you must look into Waldorf education." So she came back to Baltimore and said to us, we must look into Waldorf education. And the other teacher and I said, "Great." We were committed to being very eclectic, so we just thought it was one more ingredient for the soup pot. What we found was that everything we brought the children out of Waldorf they just opened to so much more deeply than in everything else we were bringing to them. And I kept thinking, "what is this that they're experiencing, that they're recognizing?" We liked what we saw at Waldorf. But I don't think alone we would have realized how extraordinary this was; it was really the children. (1999)

Esoteric fairs, spiritual communities, star charts, and mystical moments; these could be the stuff of satire and stereotype, except that in each case the person interviewed credits these experiences with profound changes in the direction of his or her life. I have interviewed enough persons to know that members of the older generation of schools do not speak this way; Al Tomlinson took a conventional math class with Dr. von Baravalle and ended up becoming a Waldorf teacher (1999). George Rose filled in when the Garden City school needed a music teacher and found a career (1996). Lucy Schneider sent her children to the Steiner School in New York and gradually became interested in working there (1999). It is possible, of course, that older Waldorf teachers had equally esoteric experiences but held them in confidence during our interviews. If this is the case, then at least the fact of the openness with which members of the Alternative generation speak represents a change from the past. Their accounts strike my ear (leaving aside colloquialisms and modern culture) like the accounts of those who experienced "awakenings" earlier in U.S. history. And their clash with their elders (who were, in retrospect, no less enlightened or awakened, but who carried themselves and expressed themselves differently) seems to follow a pattern that recurs in our history.

Parents

As part of my research, I mailed 175 questionnaires to independent and public Waldorf schools. Thirty-two schools, all independent, returned questionnaires, and the results make clear that, generally speaking, although anthroposophists founded earlier schools, later independent schools tended to be founded by interested parents. "Anthroposophists" here simply include those who, interested in the educational work of Rudolf Steiner, pursued a school founding not necessarily because they wished to teach in such a school, nor because they had children whom they wished to attend such a school, but because they saw the existence of such a school as a good thing. Of the schools founded in 1972 or earlier, parents founded only one, the Waldorf School of Baltimore. And even this is a special case. The school grew out of a commune or "intentional" residence called "Savitria." The school was founded for children of members of the community, but also in accordance with the beliefs and practices of the residents of the community. Of the remaining twenty-four schools, only four were not founded by parents. This shift is difficult to explain. Perhaps the established Waldorf schools have tended to attract to their communities anthroposophists who might otherwise establish schools where none exist, leaving "outsiders," largely parent groups, to establish new schools. Although the initiative for new schools tends to come from parents, we may note that in most cases these parents have sought help, onsite and offsite, from teacher training centers, established Waldorf schools, and experienced Waldorf teachers. These resources simply were not generally available before the 1970s, requiring those intending to start a Waldorf school to rely more on their own knowledge; requiring, that is, that they be first anthroposophists, loosely defined.

A Skeptic

Dorit Winter, former student and teacher at the Steiner School in New York City; former teacher in Great Barrington, Massachusetts; and director of Waldorf teacher training in San Francisco, is skeptical of the value of my interpretation according to generations. Not that there haven't been qualitatively different generations, but that the values that make a school a Waldorf school cut across these:

> I believe Waldorf schools appeal to people who are looking for a certain something for their children, and I don't believe that this something is European or American. The difficulty is that what is actually there in the school is not easily accepted. If you have as many Waldorf schools as there are in Europe, and as many successful graduates, you're past the critical mass in terms of visibility of the schools and the population. We haven't reached that here in the United States. The problem is that in order to send your child to a school that is culturally unknown to you requires a real dedication to something you're seeking. This will get more pervasive, this thirst for what the school offers. I don't believe this is a question of class, race, or ethnicity. I believe it's a soul-spiritual question. What Waldorf schools offer is delicate and hard to articulate or package.
>
> I don't believe low enrollments exist because schools are too Eurocentric. Our ideals don't yet speak to this country in a way the people who are looking for those ideals know where to find them.

I believe that is going to change, and has started to change in California. The growth in the number of Waldorf schools shows this.

The parents who enter teacher training have a tremendous awareness of the human values a child gets in a Waldorf school. In a society where values come from video games, movie screens, and the Internet, people who are squeezed by life circumstances do not have the luxury of considering values in life. The human values in a Waldorf school are therefore elitist, not because you can't find a man who has a menial job and has no sense of values in life. But can he find us and can we support him if he doesn't have the money to send his child?

If every school were endowed with all the money needed to have any child in the school, the whole picture would change. Having money and having human values don't necessarily go together because materialism closes you off from a realization that there's more to life than material assets. Humanity as a whole has always consisted of very few people, elitist as that sounds. There are few people who have a sense for the values of art and morality, truth, beauty and goodness—those are our standards, our yardsticks, our goals. Who has those values anymore? Perhaps in the future we will have these kinds of values, but not all parents have them. The parents who have this tremendous awe and reverence for a school are a small group. (Winter 1999)

While acknowledging the durability of values regarding, for example, art and morality, we must—as Winter would—acknowledge changes or evolution in their manifestation. To the extent that these changes may be categorized according to generations, and to the extent that people seeking them express their search in a particular cultural context, my interpretation holds.

Transitions

My description of generations has not regarded the transition from one to the next. Transitions sometimes take the form of rebellion; that is, Americans seeking to make something their own; youth asserting itself against age; but they also involve accommodation. Each new generation must compromise with the past and orient itself toward the promise of the future. The strengths of each generation are available to those following, even if they are disdained. The "Europeans" (yes, they were Americans, but they looked to Europe for their model) established a Waldorf school in New York City, including a curriculum and an institutional organization and culture. Whatever feelings the Americans had for the generation before them, they were indebted to it for the grist it provided for their mills. Taylor-Weaver is clear, however, that the Europeans, watching what became of their project in the hands of upstart Americans, drew back and did not provide all the assistance of which they felt capable. They were loath to transmit their wisdom to those whom they found wanting (Private communication, April 1998).

Similarly, Dorit Winter's lecture at an AWSNA conference in Toronto in 1999 offers a powerful argument with regard to the transition between the Americans and the Alternatives. Part of her lecture addressed what she called the "missing" generation in Waldorf schools, the generation that came of age in the 1960s. This generation was not missing warm bodies—many Waldorf teachers at and after the turn of the 21st century are part of the post-war baby boom. It was missing a direct historical connection with the generation of teachers and anthroposophists that had preceded it. Winter, daughter of an anthroposophist and a former Steiner School student, believes that the excesses of experimentation in the late 1960s and early 1970s "derailed" many in her cohort. Rather than apprenticing themselves to older, more experienced teachers, they found their way to Waldorf school teaching and anthroposophy by alternate routes (Winter 1999).

Although I have used specific schools and dates to illustrate my generational divisions, these should in no way be seen as fixed, or as clearly marked as I may have made them out to be. Different schools fit my general model in different ways. Schools of older generations gradually take on characteristics of the new, while simultaneously clarifying what will become the future.

4. THE SOCIAL MISSIONARIES

EVENTUALLY, WALDORF SCHOOLS WILL HAVE SATURATED their possible markets as independent alternatives to public education. There are, depending on how you count, about 4000 Montessori schools in the United States, and that number seems unlikely to grow. Further, the first Waldorf school was founded to educate the children of factory-workers' children. Ida Oberman finds evidence that this was a com-promise—Emil Molt funded a school for these children, and funding was not available then for a school for more bourgeois children. But Steiner's lectures also refer to the "forward thinking" of the "working class."

The number of independent Waldorf schools may grow, but Waldorf education has begun to appear in public education. Despite opposi-tion from within and from without, it will likely continue to grow within public systems. Opposition from within comes from those who see compromise with "the state," meaning governments from the most local to the federal, as a threat.

Often, these criticisms are attributed to the authority of remarks Steiner made regarding state intervention in education in Germany following World War I. It seems clear, however, that Prussian law, a cen-tralized ministry of education, and state school inspectors have little relation to U.S. school systems, which have always been controlled primarily by local school boards and funded by local property taxes. And, to take a larger view, as Henry James (2008) said, "...one might enumerate the items of high civilization, as it exists in other countries, which are absent from the texture of American life... No State, in the European sense of the word..."

Opposition from without comes from those, like Dan Dugan and PLANS (People for Legal and Nonsectarian Schools), who oppose what they see as a religious incursion into appropriately nonsectarian public schools. This question is addressed in more detail below.

Despite these oppositions, the last two decades have seen the introduction of Waldorf education into public school systems, usually in the form of charter schools, but, in one case, so far unique, simply as a choice within a larger system. This school, the Milwaukee Urban Waldorf School, is the first example of the contemporary generation that I will examine.

A second example of this generation is an independent school, but an independent school unlike others I have encountered. It serves the Oglala Sioux or Lakota people on the Pine Ridge Reservation, South Dakota, and is funded entirely from external sources; that is, through philanthropy or charity, and not at all through tuition, fees, or other local revenue.

These two schools, different in many respects but similar in some important ones, represent a new generation of Waldorf education. The Milwaukee school is large (more than 300 students in grades K through 6), urban, and public. The Wolakota school is tiny (21 children in grades K and 3 in 2002; just early childhood in 2010), rural, and independent. The Milwaukee school was founded in 1991, and the Wolakota school in 1993. More important to the future, both of these schools serve underprivileged, impoverished, or lower working class minority families and students. In this they are unique among Waldorf schools in the United States, and face challenges that other Waldorf schools, whether independent or charter, do not. Both schools have morning and noon meal programs, for example. Each of these schools must also adapt a "Waldorf" curriculum to serve minority families. The Milwaukee school is 98 or 99 percent African American; therefore, it chooses and adapts songs, verses, music, stories, and myths to reflect an African American heritage. (At this school I heard little talk of "multiculturalism" or its cousins, such as "cultural pluralism." The mission of the school plainly includes the development and enrichment of an African American heritage. This is not to say that European or white culture is excluded, but that there is a deliberate emphasis on black experience.) The Wolakota school serves 95 percent Lakota families, and is consciously working to preserve Lakota traditions. The founders of the school clearly believed Waldorf education would allow them to pursue this goal.

I was tempted to define a difference here by comparing the continuous and relatively uninterrupted tradition of the Lakota with the more constructed and discontinuous traditions of African Americans; but, on reflection, I find that this distinction doesn't hold up. Despite terrible oppression, important aspects of African culture have survived in black communities; and, from another point of view, all culture is a continual debate between memories of the past and demands of the present. There is no longer a pristine Lakota culture; it, too, must be revived, reconstructed, and re-imbibed in the face of pressures from more conventional, white-dominated culture.

Because these schools and Waldorf charter schools consciously attempt to address the "social mission" of Waldorf education (that is, not to neglect families that cannot afford private school tuition), I call this generation the Social Missionaries. (Even those who oppose public Waldorf schools can embrace the need for reconsideration of a social mission for Waldorf education; a prime example of this is Gary Lamb's *The Social Mission of Waldorf Education.*)

The Milwaukee Urban Waldorf School

Locate the impressive Milwaukee Art Museum sailing into Lake Michigan, on the shoreline drive and shadowed by downtown Milwaukee. Now drive straight west, away from the lake, away from money and away from the Midwest. The African-Americans who largely inhabit the "inner city" of Milwaukee still speak with the southern accents of their grandparents and great-grandparents, blacks who came north in the Great Migration to escape the memories of slavery, the bigotry of the south, the rural poverty of the depression. In a neighborhood of run-down but habitable row houses, Christian churches of many Protestant sects, and check-cashing holes-in-the-wall, you will find a modern school building, brick with bright tile accents, the Milwaukee Urban Waldorf School. (Since I wrote this, the school has relocated to an older, larger building in order to expand through eighth grade.) It is the only Waldorf school in the United States that is, simply, a public school. It is not a "charter" school, and does not receive money from student vouchers. It houses around 310 students, 98 or 99 percent African-American, in grades K–5. Like many urban schools but unlike most Waldorf schools in the United States, children may eat breakfast before school and stay long afterward in "wraparound" programs. It is one of about 115 public elementary schools in the Milwaukee district, a "specialty" school in a "choice" program, created by forward thinkers in Milwaukee in 1991. Other choice schools include schools that use Montessori methods, schools that emphasize the educational use of technology, and "immersion" schools that teach in Spanish, French, German, or sign language.

A paragraph in a school selection guide published by the school district describes the school this way: "Urban Waldorf follows a year-round calendar using a trimester system with three breaks during the year and no school during the month of July. Its curriculum reflects the phases of child development. Concepts are expanded through movement, music, recitation, visual arts, and traditional reading, writing and math. Waldorf methods develop clarity of thought, sensitivity of feeling, and strength of will. Specially-trained Waldorf teachers stay with their class groups as they move through the grades."

Unlike independent Waldorf schools, Urban Waldorf is required to give standardized tests, and they were being administered during the week I visited. Several faculty members characterized the students, apologetically, as "on edge" because of the tests, but nearly every student I saw was exceptionally well-behaved and courteous. A third grade teacher said that the two weeks of testing were disruptive but "a small price to pay" for being able to teach the way she wanted to teach the rest of the year. Teachers were exceptionally attentive to their students, and I had no sense that this was caused by my presence. Mark Birdsall, then "implementer"—a paid liaison between the Milwaukee public school system and the Association of Waldorf Schools of North America (AWSNA)—at the school, described this attentiveness as usual and necessary because of the behavioral and emotional difficulties that some students suffered. "Things can get out of hand pretty quickly," he said. Laura Birdsall, a fourth grade teacher, characterized her class as having half the students working up to grade level, and including three cognitively disabled and four learning disabled students in a class of twenty-one. She also described a student who had suffered horrific abuse—being doused with boiling water—at home. Teachers monitored students more closely than in any school I have seen. Absence required a letter from home upon return. Teasing was shut down instantly. Speech was monitored as in this exchange during a time when children were working quietly at their desks:

> Student: "He sharpening his pencil."
> Teacher (calmly): "He is...?"
> Student: "He is sharpening his pencil."
> Teacher (matter-of-fact): "Standard English."

The faculty of the Urban Waldorf School is about half African-American. Administrators believe it would be better—not that it isn't acceptable as is—to have more black teachers, but trained Waldorf teachers of color are few and far between. Except for a group trained at the founding of the school, few exist. The school hopes, with a charter Waldorf school nearby (the Tamarack School) and the Prairie Hill Waldorf School, half an hour west of Milwaukee, to implement a new round of training soon. In the meantime, the school has to accept teachers, white and black, who will get on-the-job training and begin to employ Waldorf methods as they learn them. Among these teachers, attitudes vary regarding Waldorf methods, according to those with whom I spoke. One teacher I observed, able, kind, and diligent, did not say a morning verse with her class, for example, although the curriculum she followed would have been recognizable to Waldorf teachers anywhere in the United States. (Saying a prayer-like morning verse is a universal custom among Waldorf schools.)

The school owes its existence, initially, to Mark Stamm, Robert Peterkin, and Mary Bills. Stamm, a former student at the University of Wisconsin, Milwaukee (UWM), and an anthroposophist, who proved impossible to track down for an interview, suggested to Superintendent Peterkin, now at Harvard's Graduate School of Education, that Milwaukee ought to include a Waldorf school as one of the choices among its schools. Peterkin investigated and approved, supported by Mary Bills, then president of the Milwaukee school board. Ann Pratt, an experienced Waldorf teacher from New Hampshire, took on a role as liaison or "implementer" to facilitate communication between the largely independent world of Waldorf education in the United States and the Milwaukee public school bureaucracy and to aid in training Milwaukee public school teachers in Waldorf methods. In this she was assisted by Betty Staley, an experienced Waldorf teacher and teacher at Rudolf Steiner College in Fair Oaks, California and Francis Vig, a teacher at the Chicago Waldorf School. Belden Paulsen, a professor at UWM, made possible an accredited training, and Dorothy St. Charles, a public school teacher at the time, stepped up to become the first principal of the school.

I asked Paulsen why Milwaukee, of all places, should be the first—and so far only—public district to open a Waldorf school. He characterized Milwaukee as having its fair share of conservative segregationist racists, but cited the city's progressive tradition. The mayors of Milwaukee from 1948 to 1960, for example, had been socialists, he said. More importantly, he ascribed the success of the school to "a few creative, innovative individuals," and emphasized his belief that change can be accomplished by a few key people.

He saw no reason why many large public school districts couldn't adopt a choice system similar to Milwaukee's, and include within it a school or two that uses Waldorf methods. On the other hand, he quoted a teacher from the early days saying that Waldorf teaching wasn't "simply a job; it's a way of life." The demands of Waldorf teaching, especially including training time and expenses beyond those required for regular school certification, could be daunting, if not prohibitive. He recalled that the school received a dozen or so calls from school districts as far away as California and Texas, but that early interest never amounted to much. He characterized outside interest as relatively superficial; without a commitment specifically to Waldorf educational methods, it seemed, the effort required to implement such a school was too great.

I asked Cheryl Colbert, a former teacher at the school and now principal, about accusations of racism or Eurocentrism regarding Waldorf education. She, an African-American, claimed these were not an issue for her or for the school. "I don't know where Steiner got them," she said, "but storytelling, music, movement... these are part of the African tradition, and they're good for children."

I attended a Black History Month assembly at the school. In some ways it was like Waldorf school assemblies everywhere. Children entered by classes, generally quietly, and sat in neat rows on the gym floor. Several students, led by a teacher, played music at the front of the room. A teacher stood to lead the assembly and introduce the performers. The differences were in the culture of the school. The initial music was African drumming. The assembly leader used a microphone, and was more flamboyant than other (white) Waldorf teachers I have seen. Many of the presentations would not have seemed out of place at any Waldorf school—students reciting poetry, for example—while others definitely expressed the rhythm and music of Africa and an African-American heritage. The assembly ended with the school's theme song, more like a midwestern school anthem than the lyrical stuff you might hear at other (coastal) Waldorf schools.

For many Waldorf teachers and for the Association of Waldorf Schools of North America (AWSNA), a public school cannot be a Waldorf school; it can only claim to be "Waldorf-inspired." I find little evidence to support making such a distinction in Steiner's work. In fact, Nancy Parsons Whittaker quotes Steiner as saying that his methods may be applied "anywhere there is the will to do it" (2001). AWSNA's argument would surely be that any school or teacher can use Steiner's methods, but only in an independent school can teachers work freely "out of anthroposophy," and only in this case can a school consider itself a Waldorf school. Other than providing a label for parent consumption, if you will, the distinction seems facile to me; a child's experience at the Milwaukee Urban Waldorf School is the experience of an education according to Steiner's educational principles. Some teachers are anthroposophists and some are not; some teachers are skilled and committed, others are not; but these statements are true for private Waldorf schools as well.

Frankly, under Dorothy St. Charles' leadership, the school seemed to have achieved a remarkable degree of independence. Ms. St. Charles relates several stories regarding curricular decisions that she and her faculty were able to make as a school against the recommendations of the Milwaukee district administration. For instance, the school used Waldorf methods to teach reading and writing in first and second grade; it did not use "canned" reading programs produced by textbook publishers. At a back-to-school meeting for principals each summer (the city of Milwaukee has about 115 schools within the district), the superintendent introduced new textbooks and programs. Each year, St. Charles declined to adopt them, with the superintendent's approval. After a few years, St. Charles said, all eyes would turn to her when the new program was announced. Others knew she would decline it.

I asked St. Charles what the biggest challenge to implementing Waldorf education in a Milwaukee public schools had been, and her answer surprised me: "Grievances from the teachers' union," she said. Waldorf school teachers meet weekly, and union agreements restricted teachers to one faculty meeting per month. Although all the teachers at the Urban Waldorf School had agreed to meet weekly, their union filed grievances on their behalf for breach of contract. I wondered how these were resolved. "I don't really know. They simply went away," St. Charles said. (2001) They were filed and forgotten, and the teachers continued to meet weekly.

There may be more freedom available to those in public schools than private Waldorf school teachers or AWSNA representatives may believe. And the degree of freedom likely has as much to do with those involved (superintendent, school board, principal, teachers, and parents) as with the law. Although private Waldorf schools espouse a philosophy of freedom, the pressure on new and young teachers, especially, to hew to the school culture is strong; and many who leave teaching at a private Waldorf school in their first years might scoff at the idea that they enjoyed greater freedom than their peers at another school. (Teacher attrition in Waldorf schools, as it is for almost all schools, is about 50 percent within the first three years.)

As George Hoffecker, a former private Waldorf school teacher, who became principal at the first Waldorf charter school in California and is now retired, says, the difference between public and private Waldorf schools lies primarily in the compromises a teacher is willing to make. Private schools make economic compromises, especially in educating primarily those who can afford tuition; and public schools make political compromises with federal, state, and local law, and with the community of the school.

Eugene Schwartz draws a distinction between Waldorf and Waldorf-inspired schools in that laws regarding the separation of church and state (or perhaps better stated, against the state establishment of religion) mean that students in public schools, regardless of teaching method, do not, for example, include the name "God" in their morning verse.

This seems a somewhat nominalist and picayune point; whether or not a teacher or a student is allowed to speak a word or not seems to have little bearing on inner attitude or pedagogical experience. Some of us manifest reverence without naming it; and others may talk about it all the time without once experiencing it.

Schwartz's view may simply not be correct, either; the Pledge of Allegiance and U.S. currency name God, and although these may be contested expressions, they have (so far) not been seen as government establishment of religion. The wording of the Constitution is clear, but interpretation is contested over time. As Dorothy St. Charles found, a lot depends on the community of the school.

This is not to say that the issue of religion and Waldorf education is a simple one. The field extends, minimally, over three points of view. The first might be that all education, all meaningful human endeavor, has, in the broadest sense, a religious component. As A.N. Whitehead (1929/1967) said, "The essence of education is that it be religious" (14). To speak of value, explicitly or implicitly, is to give evidence of a religious engagement with the world. This view is too broad to consider here, however, and does not necessarily distinguish Waldorf education from other methods.

The second point of view, probably the source of Waldorf critics' frustration with aspects of Waldorf education as manifested by certain teachers or, potentially, by certain schools, is that Waldorf education is religious in a more conventional sense because some ideologues, through misunderstanding and misapplication of Steiner's work, make it so.

The third point of view, and the more carefully considered, is that Waldorf education and anthroposophy, the method that underlies it, are not religions at all. Douglas Sloan, former coordinator of the joint program in Religion and Education between Union Theological Seminary and Teachers College, Columbia University, New York, made this point eloquently as an expert witness in a lawsuit arguing that charter Waldorf schools, as religious schools, violate the First Amendment of the U.S. Constitution. Sloan (2004) argued against this view:

> By all scholarly criteria of what constitutes religion, anthroposophy is not a religion....

The attempt to define religion has been notoriously difficult, and the approaches to doing so are many. In general there have been three main approaches.

The first can perhaps be called the *essentialist* approach. Essentialist definitions tend to focus on the inner essence or substance, the metaphysical reality claims, of religions, and the relationships to these demanded of human beings by the claimed realities. One of the conceptual difficulties with this focus is that philosophers and others can make metaphysical and ethical arguments about the nature of reality without advancing these as themselves constituting a religion, although they may well have implications for religion.

The second main approach to the study and definition of religion can be called the *functional* approach, and is probably the theoretical approach most favored by social scientists, although as I shall point out, some theologians also favor it. Functional definitions of religion stress the effects, the functions of religion, in actual life—the ways in which religion functions to fulfill basic human needs, both individually and communally. Different scholars stress different functions as the defining characteristic of religion. Among these various functional definitions are, for examples: the *cognitive*—religion provides meaning systems for understanding and coping with life; the *psychological*—religion functions to meet psychological needs, such as, a sense of security in the face of life's uncertainties, a sense of identity, a sense of purpose, and so forth; the *social*—religion serves primarily to provide values for social cohesion and the preservation of the social group; and the *ideological* (Marxist definitions of religion are a good example)—religion serves the power interests of governing elites by deluding the masses. Each of these taken by itself is decidedly reductionist, and, in order to avoid inordinate reductionism, most scholars attempt to fashion combinations of various functional approaches.

One form of functionalism, often utilized by students of religion, is that of the twentieth-century American theologian, Paul Tillich. Religion Tillich defined as expressing "the ultimate concern" of an individual or of an entire culture. Every person and every society, he argued, has its "ultimate concern" (often, to be sure, directed toward less than ultimate objective realities).

In fact, for Tillich, every culture is grounded in its own ultimate concern, to which it gives concrete expression. Culture itself as a whole is, therefore, *the* religious expression and activity par excellence.

"Religion," Tillich famously wrote, "is the substance of culture, culture is the form of religion." Tillich's position can be a good illustration of how the strength of the functionalist can also be its main weakness. The strength is that it enables one to see the religious functions, as noted above, of many human activities not usually recognized as religious: the state, the university, science, technology, the stock exchange, Sunday afternoon football, and so on. Each has its ultimate concern, and often its own "priesthood," paths of initiation, dogmas, sacred texts, and other marks of religion.

The weakness is that a definition which begins to apply to everything often ends up telling us little about anything.

In view of these various approaches, it is not surprising that one leading historian of American religion (Catherine Albanese of UC Santa Barbara), whose works I reviewed in forming my opinion, has observed that scholars have become increasingly less certain about what should be counted as religion as a general phenomenon. "In the end," she writes, "religion is a feature that encompasses *all* of human life, and therefore it is difficult if not impossible to define it."

In this light it is probably also not surprising that historians of religion turn mainly to the third approach to the definition of religion, namely, the *formal*. Scholars in the history of religion and comparative religion deal primarily with the actual religious forms manifested by concrete religious groups and movements. These religious forms include such things as beliefs and doctrines (creeds), ritual activities, forms of worship, sacred texts, and recognized sources of authority. The advantage and strength of this approach is that it is concrete and makes it possible to determine whether a group actually functions, not just religiously in general, a la Paul Tillich, for instance, but as a formal, identifiable religion as such. It also is possible then to distinguish it in detail from other religions and their forms, and to trace the actual development of a specific religion over time. In this perspective, a religious group is one that manifests and is organized around these common religious forms, albeit with its own distinct versions of them. This approach can also incorporate aspects of the first two approaches.

It is especially from the perspective of this third approach to the definition of religion, the formal, that I can meaningfully and concretely testify that anthroposophy is not a religion....

Anthroposophy is the name given by Rudolf Steiner to designate the way of knowing, the method of inquiry, that he established....

It is a wholly personal choice not only whether one follows Steiner's method of knowing and tries to develop it, but also whether, out of conviction, one accepts—or does not—Steiner's own results and content flowing from that method as he practiced it. If the principle of individual freedom based on knowledge is violated in following Steiner's indications, then the entire method is vitiated.

A Head Start

One Milwaukee first grader was so pleased with his work—copying a sentence from the blackboard: "Mufaro had two girls, one sweet and one sour."—that he held his paper before his face and kissed it. According to conventional Waldorf wisdom, the teaching of writing in first grade would be too soon. Standards (and a minority community that embraces those standards as necessary to ensure so far as possible a decent education) require teachers to accelerate the curriculum. Teachers in Milwaukee, however, are acutely aware of the compromises they must make to succeed as an "inner city" public school, and they work very hard to convey, for example, the artistry from which written letters arose historically, before they begin writing.

The Wolakota Waldorf School, Pine Ridge Reservation, South Dakota

It is true that most Waldorf schools in the United States are relatively wealthy independent schools, but there is a growing number of public and charter Waldorf schools. Not all Waldorf schools fit these two categories, however. In order to see a different school altogether, I visited the Wolakota Waldorf School on the Pine Ridge Reservation.

Drive southeast from Rapid City, South Dakota, on Route 44, down into the Cheyenne River valley, past the ranches on the plateaus above the river, on poor land that will soon look rich by comparison with the near desert given to the Lakota people of the Pine Ridge Reservation. Pass through Scenic, South Dakota, the last, depressed storefronts before the reservation, and pass within sight of the rock castles of the Badlands in their Roadrunner-and-Wile E. Coyote strangeness. Now you're on the "the rez" itself. The herds of shaggy beef cattle and blunt-nosed, round-bellied horses, animals that ignore the low barbed-wire fences that line the roads, belong to Lakota ranchers. The rolling, treeless hills trick an east-coast eye. Is that next ridge half a mile away, or five miles? Oncoming headlights appear minutes before you pass an old truck, Lakota men seated three abreast, gone at 70 mph—140 if you add your own speed to theirs. Small ash trees, cottonwoods, and scruffy pines huddle and snake through creases between the hills.

The Pine Ridge Reservation is only a bit smaller than Massachusetts—minus Cape Cod—about fifty miles north to south and 100 miles east to west. Depending on whom you ask, the population is between 15,000 and 30,000 people. The U.S. government census of 1990 lists a smaller figure of little more than 12,000, but two Lakota men with whom I spoke emphasized the larger number. Many of the Lakota, they claimed, lead semi-nomadic lives, lives that stretch from Alberta to Nevada, and that disdain the white distinctions among reservations, states, and nations such as Canada and the United States. Further, suspicion of the government certainly leads to underreporting and to a lack of faith that any attempt is really made to obtain an accurate number. A smaller number, they claim, means fewer dollars for the reservation from the Bureau of Indian Affairs (BIA).

Turn left at the convenience store in Sharp's Corner, and drive eight miles to Kyle (*Pejuta Haka*, "Medicine Root," in Lakota). Trailers, shacks, and small houses, some old, some new, are scattered like dice over the landscape. Many have half a dozen old cars, scavenged for parts, up on blocks or down in mud and frost, littering the yards. A halo of old tires, clothes lines (laundry sideways in the wind) and children's toys around each house soon gives way to the relentless rise and fall of the grassy hills. Oddly, the untidiness of this rural poverty can't compete with the bed of landscape and sheet of sky; what would be eyesores elsewhere are swallowed by the majesty of the land. People with an astonishing gift for painting and sculpture easily ignore the junkyard aesthetic of their own homes. (On the other hand, describing white people's impressions of the rez, John Haas said, "You see 'Dances With Wolves' and think, 'How beautiful!' You wouldn't mind driving around. But a week of driving 200 miles a day will change your mind." It's seventy miles or so to the nearest supermarkets, in Rapid City.)

A right on a rutted dirt road puts you within sight of the Wolakota Waldorf School: two trailers, one doublewide, the other not. Three vans, one of which works, a Ford, a Dodge and a Chevy (effectively preventing part-swapping that might make life a bit easier) are parked before the west side of the main building. On the wall is a medicine wheel, a circle enclosing a cross, about eight feet in diameter, painted in traditional colors, black, red, yellow, and white. Four directions, four winds, four races of people.

The trailer opens into a main room, which serves as classroom, dining room, and kitchen in one. Off one end are a larder, the bathroom, and an office. Off the other, the teacher's bedroom. (Six students attended the school in 2001, three in kindergarten and three in first grade. This number was to grow to 21 the following year, then fall in 2003. Since then, some years the school has had no enrollment, some years a few students, depending on teachers and resources.) The kindergarten teacher, who lives at the school, is a white man named Christopher Young (who is, incidentally, my half-brother). He attended Waldorf schools himself on the east coast (the Hawthorne Valley School and The Waldorf School of Garden City) and had some observation and student-teaching experience before he took the job in South Dakota. The first grade teacher lives nearby with his family. His name is Reggie Little Killer. He is a Lakota man, a Marine veteran, and a Mormon. He believes strongly in Waldorf education, he says, but has little experience of it and virtually no training in its methods.

School comes with breakfast and lunch. There is no tuition. Unemployment runs between 75 percent and 85 percent on the Reservation, and most families clearly cannot afford to pay even a small tuition. The teachers are paid $10,000 to $12,000 per year from money raised primarily in Europe, especially in Germany and Switzerland. Some summers, Mr. Young or Mr. Little Killer travel to Europe with photographs of the school, visiting various Waldorf schools, raising money. Isabel Stadnick (wife of Lakota Bob Stadnick, deceased, one of the founders of the Wolakota Waldorf School) also raises money in Switzerland for the school. The school also receives small contributions from some Waldorf schools in the United States, and is planning a more concerted fundraising effort.

The Pine Ridge Reservation, I hear, attracts a large number of central and northern European tourists in the summer (I was there in bleak February). Many come for a "spiritual" experience they cannot seem to find in Europe but that they believe lives strongly in the native Americans and the austere land of the rez. A Swedish woman camped alone on a butte, vision-questing. It's something of a joke to the Lakota, for many of whom spirituality is simply not something foreign or exotic. I was impressed, for example, by the effortless, seamless expression of prayer before a conference I attended and before each meal. Everyone stands, and someone is asked to say a prayer. The prayers I heard were an easy combination of Lakota tradition (mention of the Great Spirit, grandparents before us and grandchildren after us) and Protestant Christianity (ad hoc, "traveling mercies" for those attending, and thanks for the gifts around us). Some were in English, some in Lakota. Some ended with "Amen," some with the Lakota words *Mi'takuye' Oya's'in*, "All of my relations." Before sitting, many Lakota add the phrase, *Oh han*, expressing agreement with what had just been said. If the Lakota have formulaic, written, memorized prayers, I did not hear them.

In the late 1980s, several Lakota people, including John Haas, Lemoine Pulliam, Robert Stadnick, and Ermina Red Owl, active in local schools but suspicious of involvement with the elected tribal Council, believed there had to be a better way to educate children. Dropout rates at the public schools on the rez were approximately 70 percent. Schools, under Federal law, could not acknowledge Lakota spiritual traditions, which would conflict with the "establishment of religion" clause of the first amendment to the U.S. Constitution. And as money found its way from the BIA through the tribal Council to the schools, it was allegedly funneled off by rampant corruption of elected and appointed school officials and others. School governance, spirituality, and teaching and learning. In each of these areas, these people believed, there had to be a better way to educate children. And in their research, according to John

Haas, the one name that cropped up again and again was "Waldorf." So, knowing relatively little beyond what they had read, they founded the Wolakota Waldorf Society.

Robert Stadnick, school custodian at the public Little Wound School in Kyle; Norman Underbaggage, a lawyer; and Richard Moves Camp, a medicine man from nearby Wanbli, South Dakota, traveled to Dornach, Switzerland, to research Waldorf education. There they met with Dr. Heinz Zimmerman, head of the Pedagogical Section of the Anthroposophical Society, who was "extremely enthusiastic about the idea" of a Waldorf school on the reservation, according to a promotional pamphlet produced by Mr. Stadnick. This trip raised money for the school, as well, which then opened in 1993. The small school began with only a kindergarten, but the founders hoped it would find support in the community and grow quickly through twelve grades.

Climb a small hill behind the school, less than two hundred yards, and you can see the rocky spine of a ridge half a mile to the south, beyond the school and the track of the road. Hills roll for miles to the north. East, one small house. Little else. The wind drives ice before it, and provides the only sound. At your feet, another medicine wheel, about eighteen inches in diameter, made of small rocks and pebbles. In the center, wrapped in red cloth tied at the ends, like hard candies, are ceremonial offerings, probably tobacco. Here, in what is literally the backyard of the Waldorf school, people used to come on vision quests. Again, I am struck by the nearness to the road, the school, the town. Spirituality is part of life here, not distant in space or in mind. I walk down the hill, away from the tiny acropolis of this struggling school.

A Second Visit

At the invitation of the Wolakota Waldorf School, I returned to participate in a teacher-training workshop in 2002. I remained after the conference to see the school in operation. The day I observed was typical in most respects. The school has three teachers now: Susan Bunting, an experienced, trained kindergarten teacher from England and then Vermont; Christopher Young (mentioned earlier); and Edwin Around Him, a jack-of-all-trades who teaches Lakota language and culture. There is talk of, eventually, converting the school into a Lakota immersion school. (Reggie Little Killer discovered that teaching was not the career for him, and has moved on.) The school has grown from six to twenty-one students in kindergarten and third grade. Mr. Young, in good Waldorf tradition, has remained with the class that he started with in first grade. Because money and teachers were lacking, this means there are no first or second grades. Mr. Young and Ms. Bunting are certain that, with funding, they could add first and second (and next year, third) grades. They have a small pool of talented and interested local people, two Lakota and one white, who would be willing to teach, and many families who would send students to the school. Mr. Young and Ms. Bunting are in the middle of a fundraising campaign, based on a poster and a letter from the school, and their joy was obvious at receiving a $100 donation from a medical doctor on the East Coast the day I observed. They presently run the school, including instructional salaries, on $32,000 per year, or about $75 per day excluding salaries.

Their day begins before 6:00 am, putting classrooms in order for the day, and by 7:15 Mr. Young left to drive an hour and a quarter bus route to pick up about two-thirds of the students (the rest are dropped off by their parents). Ms. Bunting stayed at the school to prepare breakfast for all of us. Mr. Young stopped first at a general store, an unmarked metal barn with gas pumps out front, to pick up milk. The store doesn't need a sign because everyone knows about it, Mr. Young said, and it stays in business by bootlegging alcohol from the back.

The bus route wound through the town of Kyle and surroundings. Children appeared from derelict trailers, run-down government-built housing, and small ranch houses. They were neatly but frequently underdressed, and got in the van eagerly. They obviously had much affection for Mr. Young, telling him "knock-knock" jokes and teasing him. They also were precociously aware of mainstream American culture, far from the rez, talking about movies like "The Matrix" and "Fast and Furious." Their conversation was larded with violent images ("I'll blow up that house with my bazooka."), but my overriding impression was of their sweetness and openness. They looked after each other in small ways, buckling the seat belts of younger children, offering to lend a sweater, and asked many questions about my life in Massachusetts. Given the harsh home lives and poverty from which many of the children come, they were extremely well-disciplined and mature. A calm word from a teacher was enough to still them instantly. Eleven children, about two-thirds of the possible total, got on the van. Mondays and Fridays are not well-attended, Mr. Young told me, because of family activities that may involve driving to a powwow, for example.

We returned to the school a bit after 8:30, and all the students followed Mr. Young to the top of a knoll behind the school. We stood in a circle, as they do each morning, to say the morning verse. Then Mr. Young greeted each student in Lakota. Some responded in Lakota, and some in English (all but one of the students is Lakota).

Breakfast was cold cereal and milk, sugar or honey, and fruit juice. The tables were laid immaculately, with cloth napkins and rings, and children sat to bless the meal and eat. They chatted during breakfast, the routine well-established. After breakfast, the teachers put out bins of soapy water and students cleaned and dried their own dishes; a couple of them took it on themselves to wash my dishes for me.

The kindergarten children left the table to play, which they did spontaneously and imaginatively. The two boys who had been discussing bazookas and explosions on the bus stood at a play stove cooking an imaginary meal for the rest of the class. Other students built with blocks or played with dolls.

The third grade building is a shed, really, with a classroom about fifteen by twenty feet behind an unfinished plywood alcove or mudroom off of which are an enclosed toilet and a small storage closet. Untrimmed windows look roughly north and south, and a "blackboard" is painted on the east wall. Student paintings are pinned to the walls, and some seedlings rest on a shelf near the south window. There is a sink and some storage space in the rear of the room, with a recognizable clutter of painting supplies, chalk, beeswax for modeling, crayons, and drinking mugs. The desks and chairs are hand-me downs from the local public school, or look to be, Formica and brown-painted steel. The walls are painted a cool blue. There are seven third graders.

The third graders sauntered up to their building, where they said another verse and then answered math problems that Mr. Young asked them to solve in their heads. Their abilities varied tremendously, and Mr. Young tailored his questions appropriately. He then asked for quiet and told part of the Lakota creation myth. Mr. Young spoke the names of the gods in Lakota, so it was hard for me to follow, but the story involved the creation of plants, with their differently colored flowers, and animals, with their different numbers of legs. When Mr. Young sensed attention flagging, he ended the lesson, and the students poured out for recess.

The playground consisted of a small swing, a climbing structure, and a (broken) slide. These occupied one end of a level dirt patch about twenty-five yards long and ten yards wide. In the middle was one pole of a broken volleyball set, with shreds of netting wrapped around it. The children quickly decided to play an imaginative game of tag, similar to "Red Rover," with the volleyball pole as "home base." They were remarkably uncompetitive, taking the game seriously, but not crowing about winning, losing, or rules violations. This attitude manifested throughout the day in each activity, and I take it to be part of their culture, part that has not been destroyed by the circumstances of their lives. One boy had brought a baseball and bat, and I pitched in turn to those who wanted to play. Each batted until he got one solid hit, then gave the bat to the next hitter. Older children helped younger ones hold the bat and stand properly.

Following recess, the class returned for a brief math class, and then it was time for lunch: sausages, potatoes, and mixed frozen vegetables. Several of the students drowned their food in ketchup. The routine was the same as that at breakfast, although some of the kindergarten children were noticeably tired, slumping in their chairs and having a hard time finishing their meals. (Ms. Bunting described some students living in large extended families in very small houses, and not getting to sleep until after midnight.) After lunch, the kindergarten bedded down for rest, and the third grade had painting. Once again, their mood was calm, serious, and good-humored. They were eager and helpful in setting up to paint and cleaning the room at the end of the day. A stepladder from outside the building was brushed off to provide an easel on which the teacher could demonstrate.

School ended at 2:30, and students piled into the van. Mr. Young's route was extra-long because one parent had asked him to drop his daughter off at her aunt's house, far outside of town. Mr. Young returned to the school a bit after 4:00 pm, during which time Ms. Bunting had washed the pots from lunch. They had about an hour to unwind before they cooked dinner for themselves (and me), cleaned up, maintained buildings or van or kept appointments in town, and began to prepare for the following day. The pace at which Mr. Young and Ms. Bunting worked was relaxed and deliberate, but ceaseless. While students were in the school, the teachers' focus never left them.

Monday is not a Lakota language day, so Mr. Around Him was not officially there, although he showed up at lunch time to discuss car trouble he was having. As soon as he walked through the door, he was surrounded by the younger students especially. They clung to him and gazed at his face. Mr. Around Him, in his mid-thirties, normally drives the van, but had suffered a diabetic seizure a couple of weeks before I arrived, and was awaiting a doctor's clearance to continue this work.

The day I observed was postcard-perfect, warming quickly into the 80s. Other days, the dirt roads are impassably rutted, or the van won't start. Then Mr. Young cancels school and waits, or repairs the van. There is no set number of school days, and the schedule is extremely flexible. Mr. Around Him is expected on Tuesday, Wednesday and Thursday, but lives far from town and does not have a reliable vehicle. The school runs on "Indian time," something Mr. Young seemed more content with than did Ms. Bunting; although often neither has a choice.

I realized on this second visit to the Pine Ridge Reservation that, despite my attempts at a realistic view of Native American spirituality, I had romanticized it. I had initially taken, for instance, the prayer wheels on the school building and on the top of the knoll behind the school as evidence of a worldview. Come to find out that both prayer wheel and worldview are the products of German visitors, not of the Lakota people.

Before dinner on the first day of my second visit, Edwin Around Him held a small Styrofoam bowl containing bits of each of the dishes we were to eat. We stood in a circle and he said a prayer in Lakota. Then he handed the bowl to Mr. Young and said brightly, "Now, go run up that hill!" I assumed the food would be placed at the top of the knoll as an offering to the spirits.

After dinner we walked up the hill to survey the school's land and picture plans for developing the school when more money is raised. No Styrofoam bowl in sight! A new, larger medicine wheel in a saddle between two small hills, however. I turned to Mr. Young: "You've got a new, larger medicine wheel," I said. "Yeah," he said, resignedly, "the Germans built it last summer.""And where's the bowl of food?" I asked. "Oh, around the corner of the school," he said, which meant that it was in some undergrowth near the non-working vans. "You don't take it anywhere in particular?""No, just outside." Telling Mr.Young to run up the hill had been a joke.

Here I was, continually arguing against the improper objectification of things that are not objects, coming to realize that I hadn't given the Lakota credit for the same concept. Tops of hills, medicine wheels made of stone, and small dishes of food are not the point. The land on which we were standing wasn't even Indian land until a bit over a hundred years ago when the Lakota were sent there by the white, from more fertile and arguably more beautiful land near the Black Hills. The Lakota could find a holy site, or make one, on the Pine Ridge Reservation, but if life took them elsewhere, as it had brought them here, they could do the same.

Since I wrote this in 2002, Lemoine Pulliam died (he was diabetic), and Ulrike left the reservation, likely to return to Germany. The school closed briefly after Chris Young moved to New Hampshire, but it retained its board of trustees and then re-opened as a kindergarten only.

Charter Waldorf Schools: Woodland Star, Stone Ridge, and Sebastopol

The hobbit hills north of San Francisco and Sacramento, California, are full of Waldorf schools, public and private. I drove there to visit three charter Waldorf schools during a cold spell that had Californians complaining but that felt like my Massachusetts home in spring.

I first visited the Woodland Star Charter School, in Sonoma, founded by Chip Romer and others. Chip, former owner of a San Francisco comedy club, looks a bit like John Malkovich and is affable, thoughtful, and completely committed to Waldorf education. For most, founding one Waldorf school is enough, but Chip is now in the process of founding a second school, the Credo Charter School, a Waldorf methods high school that he plans to fill with the eighth grade graduates of more than a half dozen charter Waldorf schools within commuting range, eventually to have more than 600 students. This would make it the largest school using Waldorf methods in the United States. The school is part, too, of an ambitious sustainable development that would eventually include hundreds of homes, many businesses, and be "carbon neutral."

The Credo School is yet to open, however, and Chip took me to see the Woodland Star Charter School. Woodland Star is a modest, cheerful school, housed in blue-trimmed tan modular unites provided by the local school district. Inside each unit is one classroom, and although they have a generic exterior, each interior is instantly recognizable as a Waldorf school classroom: pastel curtains, carefully painted, colorful walls; pictures and projects that demonstrate themes associated with each year (human beings and animals in fourth grade and Greek history in fifth grade, for example).

I saw a math class led by a sweet but under-prepared teacher who read verses and poems from a cheat-sheet (uncharitably, I wondered if she had been alerted to my visit and was performing as she thought she should). I also saw excellent classes in fifth and sixth grade geometry. In the fifth grade class, the teacher led the students in constructing a drawing. At one point, we were all to imagine a line coming up out of the earth, passing through the blackboard at a marked point, and then continuing on through the fourth grade classroom next door and out into the universe forever. As a boy bent over his work, a tone of discovery in his voice, he said, "I love doing this!" Finally, I visited a kindergarten class at the transition from free play to snack. One boy took my hand and showed me where to sit and how to make a "bird's nest" of my hands to receive some apple slices. The teacher sang a song about working hard and working together, and the children leapt to clean up their toys and get ready for rest time.

The children in all the classes were attentive, engaged, and well-behaved. In the second grade, coordinated waves of students quietly got water and returned to their desks, and children who had to use the restroom took a wooden pass and left the room without disrupting others, while the teacher serenely conducted a math class that included calling on each student to answer a problem that he or she had solved mentally.

The school's classrooms and administrative buildings are set among playgrounds and gardens that the school has created over the past several years. The school is an "independent" charter school, meaning that it can incorporate as a non-profit institution separate from its school district, allowing it to receive charitable contributions. The school asks for parent contributions (in addition to the $5000 to $5500 the school receives from the state per student per year), and it receives an average of about $100 per month per family. The amount the school receives from the state is the same for every charter school and varies by year based on the state budget.

As I visited classes and met students, teachers, and administrators, I asked myself the following question: If I did not know that this is a charter school, and not a private Waldorf school, would I be able to tell, and how? I would have guessed that it be easier than it was. In fact, the only discernable differences usually had more to do with socio-economic realities—the children's clothing wasn't always as expensive as it might have been at a private school—than with educational ones.

The reason I felt it necessary to ask this question has to do with objections to the introduction of Waldorf education into public or charter schools. Steiner opposed "state control" of education, and some within the world of independent Waldorf schools, particularly, it seems, those who work for the Association of Waldorf Schools of North America, see public magnet schools and charter schools as state-controlled. Such control, they believe, necessarily jeopardizes the autonomy that schools and teachers must have to be able to teach truly as they believe they ought.

It seems to me that this argument, while not entirely specious, misunderstands the word "state" as it is used in political science—to mean a centralized government, and not necessarily a province, which we in the United States call a "state" because of the history of our founding. More important, however, are two facts and one opinion. First, the United States has a long history of local control of its schools through school boards. Romer advises all charter schools to get someone from their school communities elected to their local school boards in order to better represent the views of the community; for him, it's just common sense and good politics. Second, although the federal government affects education through mandates like No Child Left Behind (NCLB), it provides relatively little funding, oversight, or enforceable consequences for such measures. Federal oversight may increase in the future—or it may decrease, opposed by many, many communities, not just Waldorf school communities.

Further, as one teacher at the Sebastopol, California, charter school said, "There's the question of whether or not the state can control a school, which it can; and then whether or not it does, which it hasn't. And if we want to fear state control, we could fear it equally in private schools, which are not immune to the law."

Another teacher, who had taught for years in an independent Waldorf school before joining the staff of the Sebastopol school, said: "The only thing I have changed in moving from private to public—the only thing—is to replace the words 'God' or 'spirit' where they appear in verses. Not in stories; these are cultural history; just in verses that we say with the children."

Her account may hold true for her classroom practice; I observed a geography lesson in which she had transformed the California state standards on teaching California geography (which would have been done in a Waldorf school in fourth grade anyway) into a dynamic exercise in which she had students play tectonic plates, valleys, mountains, rivers, and even the Pacific Ocean; but skeptics would raise the issue of testing. Surely the time devoted to test preparation and the weeks devoted to testing compromise the children's Waldorf education.

As Sheila Reilly (the administrator at the Woodland Star School) told me, however, acknowledging that the "dance between children's developmental needs and state standards" is one of the greatest challenges her school faces. "If there's a standard that we don't believe is developmentally appropriate, we ignore it." Further, the old California standards are to be replaced in the next couple of years with standards that many with whom I spoke believed would be more developmentally appropriate, easier to interpret, and more "Waldorf friendly."

Regarding the weeks devoted to testing (a two-week period in May each year for students in grades two through eight), everyone connected with public Waldorf schools believed this was a small price to pay in order to be able to serve the communities they served, communities from which few if any could afford a private school education.

Several teachers and administrators with whom I spoke also defended standards. Anne Cummings (who has taught in a public school, a private Waldorf school, and in teacher education programs, and who is now an administrator at the Woodland Star School) said, "public school standards can bring professionalism and accountability to Waldorf education." While she might quibble with testing students and with some standards and assessment, she wasn't troubled by the issue overall.

Based on students' test scores, each California school is given a score, called an Academic Performance Index (API). Schools above 800 are generally above government oversight. Sebastopol is consistently above 800. Woodland Star and Stone Ridge Charter School, in Napa, the other Waldorf charter school I visited, were not; and they fell into an area that requires annual improvement. Woodland Star had not achieved the required improvement, but, when the local district examined test scores they discovered something worth noting—something that those familiar with Waldorf education might even have predicted. Students' scores were, on average "too low" in the early grades, but significantly higher in seventh and eighth grades. Reilly explained that students are ranked from a low of one to a high of five. Not a single seventh or eighth grader was ranked in the bottom two categories. According to Reilly, this was unique in her district. To be clear, those students who, on average, had been "too low" a few years earlier had made such progress that now, in seventh and eighth grades, on average, they were out-performing their cohort in non-Waldorf schools. "A curve is rising for us that is falling in almost every other school; performance tends to decline after about fourth grade. And the district is very interested in us because of this."

Beyond the issue of testing, those who oppose or who are suspicious of the introduction of Waldorf education into public schools believe that a "free" alternative will threaten independent Waldorf school enrollment, weakening or even replacing a pure Waldorf school with something that looks a lot like one but isn't one, and one that can be controlled or adulterated by the state. Finally, some worry that there is a shortage of Waldorf school teachers in the United States; Douglas Gerwin, Co-Director of the Research Institute for Waldorf Education (REWI), in a presentation at a meeting of Waldorf teacher educators in January 2011, calculated that there are roughly 300 openings in independent Waldorf schools each year and only about 130 graduates of Waldorf teacher certification programs to fill these positions. And the movement of teachers to public schools that offer higher pay and greater benefits will only exacerbate this situation.

Regarding the apparent conflicts between public and private Waldorf schools, George Hoffecker (consultant to public Waldorf schools and former Principal of the Twin Ridges charter school, the first Waldorf charter school in the country, founded in 1993) put it succinctly: "If you want to make economic compromises, work in a private Waldorf school. If you want to make political compromises, work in a public Waldorf school" (2010). By economic compromises, he is referring primarily to the necessity of finding a community that could afford private education and ignoring those who could not. Other economic compromises, however, include low pay and the parents' "power of the pocketbook," which is the power to influence decisions at a school, ultimately, by leaving or threatening to leave; or, alternately, by funding what they believe important. By political compromises, Hoffecker is referring to making peace with uncomfortable standards and assessments, and also the necessity for teachers to be state certified.

Several charter school teachers and administrators also referred to the challenge of dual certification. There were two basic routes by which teachers enter charter Waldorf schools, and neither is easy. First, certified public school teachers can complete a Waldorf teacher certification, either before or, more usually, during their employment in a Waldorf charter school. This is time consuming and can be costly. Second, Waldorf school teachers can obtain state certification, again before, or more usually, during their employment.

Challenges exist in each category. Public school teachers sometimes "don't even know what they don't know" about the relationship of Waldorf methods to anthroposophy and the need for continual "deepening," according to one teacher. They may have too superficial a relationship to method or technique, and resist developing the capacities out of which method and technique should flow. And private school teachers may be ill-equipped for the challenges of working in a community in which many students do not speak English as a first language; in which parents are not used to supporting school life at home; in which the ideas of a dress code or a media use policy are novel; in which many students have special needs.

I met with the faculty of the Sebastopol school to discuss their experiences in making these transitions: from public to charter Waldorf, from private Waldorf to charter Waldorf. A public school teacher had found that in the public schools, workbooks, readers, and textbooks became the focus of his life. He was expected to "get the curriculum through to the children," and felt "constantly compromised" in his efforts to teach the children as individuals. Since coming to the Waldorf school he felt "far freer, with time to stop and look at each child to see what excites his or her curiosity."

Another teacher with experience in both public and private Waldorf schools replied that "innovation and freedom depend on the particular school, whether private or public." In her experience (and in that of others with whom I spoke) private Waldorf schools held no monopoly on freedom, and could be quite coercive in holding teachers to one view of a curriculum. "Every school, public or private, has a culture and the consequent pressures of that culture," she said. She was more comfortable in the public Waldorf schools because of their "social and creative mission." She found greater "questioning and innovation" in public Waldorf schools than she had in private ones.

A Different View of Charter Waldorf Schools

In order to hear more about objections to Waldorf charter schools, I had lunch with Patrice Maynard, Director of Outreach for AWSNA; I had been told she is skeptical of public Waldorf schools. She described her first encounter with Waldorf charter schools, in 1996, when she attended her first AWSNA meeting as a delegate for the independent Hawthorne Valley School. "There was a push to have charter Waldorf schools as members of AWSNA" (2010). She was concerned that "you can't have a movement toward freedom and independence when schools have ties to government." This led to her opposition to including charter or public schools in AWSNA, but doesn't reflect her view of the schools themselves. She told me, "I love that there are charter schools—they're part of my belief in the value of experimenting with Steiner's ideas." But there should initially have been more conversation between charter and independent Waldorf schools so that charter Waldorf schools (which may not always have honestly represented how "Waldorf" they were) didn't drain enrollment from independent Waldorf schools. For example, charter Waldorf schools should have stopped to ask, "How are our actions impacting others?"

Maynard believes that "charter schools should tell the truth; don't call it 'Waldorf education,' but be descriptive. For example, say, 'this many of our teachers have this kind of Waldorf teacher training.'"

Maynard also sees charter schools in general (including, but not limited to Waldorf charter schools) as a "distraction from what's really at stake," which is the possibility of an imminent confrontation between support for public education in crisis and any moves to dismantle independent schooling in general. "Public education has been shredded by textbook and curriculum companies, technology companies, pharmaceutical companies, and food service companies," according to Maynard. "Why don't charter Waldorf schools stand up to their governments, dance with the government in a way that doesn't sacrifice their integrity? Why gut the morning verse or knuckle under to testing? They've missed an opportunity for meaningful conversation." Maynard sees the work of the Foundation for Educational Choice, based on Milton Friedman's work in economics and translated into vouchers for educational choice, as leading to greater choice, greater independence for education, and, therefore, a healthier route to solving some of the apparent crises in education.

Broad and Deep

Some Waldorf teachers speak of the distinction between private and public Waldorf schools as a distinction between "deepening" (private) and "broadening" (public). According to George Hoffecker (2010), for instance, René Querido, a long-time west coast teacher educator, now deceased, opposed the introduction of Waldorf methods into public schools until he came to see the private–public movement in this way; public schools broadening or spreading the influence of Waldorf education, making it available to more and more families, and private schools deepening it, making new discoveries, finding new methods based on Steiner's principles. For Querido, a deeply religious man, these impulses formed the upright (deepening) and the crossbar (broadening) of a cross.

There's nothing particularly wrong with Querido's vision; it may contain some truth, and it may be a good way to conceptualize or rationalize some aspects of the growth of Waldorf education in the

United States. But this view is at best partial in relegating public school teachers to the role of disseminators, and handing the role of originators to those in private schools. Clearly, each teacher who engages with education fully, whether in a public school or in a private school, necessarily takes responsibility for the spread of his or her ideas or influence (a broadening); and for the source, initiative, and insight that gives birth to and accompanies these ideas or influence (a deepening).

Further, taken to an extreme, broadening without deepening is diluting; and deepening without broadening is a form of concentration that we may call ideology or even fanaticism. In the end, there is no real broadening without deepening, and vice versa. Not only do these two present a false dichotomy, they rely on one another for their mutual existence.

If we think of a source for what we call Waldorf education (and I'm not talking about the historical source, Rudolf Steiner, I'm talking about a contemporary, essential source in each teacher), it is in what I will discuss in the second part of this book as that point at which creativity, morality or ethics, and freedom meet. That point is located, potentially, in every teacher, public or private, formal or informal. To develop the intuition in each moment to provide what a student needs in the deepest sense to become increasingly human and healthy, is to engage in the free, creative, moral endeavor that we may call true education.

It is possible to take the fruits of this work, the observations and techniques that arise in the process of educating, and hand them to others to use as they see fit. In fact, this is usually what we mean by teaching, what we find in textbooks and teacher education courses. When we remember our years, even decades, of being educated, this is mostly what we endured. But when we remember our best teachers, those who influenced us most greatly, those who may even have shaped our lives or set them on a proper course, we remember not the hours of convention but the moments of insight—a sentence, a thought, an attitude or posture.

We may be tempted to think of education as a long and grueling process, one that requires a couple of years in early childhood, eight years or so in elementary school, another four of high school, perhaps four of college or university, and even years beyond that. We certainly live in a world that has constructed education in this way. Further, according to John Taylor Gatto (2002) and others, to learn to read and to write generally requires far fewer hours than we give in school. And to set a life on its path may be the work of an instant.

5. FOUR GENERATIONS, FIVE BOOKS

IN CHRONOLOGICAL ORDER, *The Recovery of Man in Childhood: A Study in the Educational Work of Rudolf Steiner* (Harwood 1958); *The Experience of Knowledge: Essays on American Education* (Gardner 1975); *Toward Wholeness: Rudolf Steiner Education in America* (Richards 1980); and *Millennial Child: Transforming Education in the Twenty-first Century* (Schwartz 1999), represent four distinct phases or generations of Waldorf education in the United States. I have chosen to call these generations "The Europeans"; "The Americans"; "The Alternatives"; and "The Social Missionaries."

These generations mirror closely (although this occurred to me years after first conceiving of them), the generalized generations of U.S. history that historians have described as "conflict," "consensus," and "plural." Very simply, many historians, led perhaps by Charles Beard (1913/1986), largely before World War II, saw historical change growing out of class conflicts as well as from political theory. Even the small presence of Waldorf schools in the United States before World War II shows evidence of this conflict view in the struggle to translate a European, especially German, working-class education for a New York Upper East Side clientele.

Consensus historians, largely after World War II, emphasized common purpose in the movement of history; for example, describing the Continental Congress as, in John P. Roche's phrase, a "reform caucus" (in Higham 1962). Similarly, having found a more or less secure footing in the United States, those who thought about Waldorf education after the War described it, for example, as offering a balance to the pendulum swings between traditional and progressive modes of education. (See Gardner 1975).

The "new" pluralistic history abjures large-scale syntheses, and throws the field open to a multi-faceted approach that includes history "from the bottom up," and consideration of previously marginalized groups (See, among others, Lemisch 1968). And, during this period, from the mid-1960s on, Waldorf schools began increasingly to portray themselves not as fellow-travelers in search of educational answers, but as (self-) marginalized institutions. Recently, since 1990 or so, Waldorf teachers and schools find themselves examining issues ranging widely from the role of Waldorf education in public school systems and juvenile corrections, to the separation of church (and school) and state. This is hard to characterize briefly. (See, for example, Smith, undated, and Oppenheimer 1999).

The ease with which Waldorf generations may be shoehorned into a simple historiography—conflict, consensus, plural—suggests two things. First, changes in historical interpretation must themselves be historicized, to consider how the practice of history reflects broader contemporaneous social concerns. And second, that the fit between my object of study (Waldorf education) and this interpretation probably calls the simplicity of that historiography into question more than it validates my descriptions.

The books I examine here do not constitute a canon in the literature of Waldorf education; rather, they are among the few works that attempt to portray Waldorf education generally for an audience that is largely unfamiliar with it. For example, three more works that might be included here are *Rudolf Steiner Education: The Waldorf Impulse* (Edmunds 1947); *Man and World in the Light of Anthroposophy* (Easton 1982); and *Insight-Imagination: The Emancipation of Thought and the Modern World* (Sloan 1983). Edmunds's work is a collection of essays written over decades. Although it appeared originally a decade before Harwood's, it is largely superseded by Harwood's more thorough investigation. The works of Easton and Sloan largely regard topics other than Waldorf education, although each book contains a chapter or an extensive appendix on Waldorf education.

Further, a large and growing body of literature examines or extends aspects of Waldorf practices, curricula, and methodologies, but works in this mode usually assume some familiarity with Waldorf education itself; that familiarity can be gained through Steiner's work, experience in Waldorf schools, or the more primary texts examined here. Although these works might be examined to tease out the historical context in which they were written, to do so would likely not add much to the discussion I will begin here.

Teachers wrote all the books examined here, although not all were teachers in Waldorf schools (M. C. Richards, author of *Toward Wholeness*, taught at Black Mountain College in North Carolina, for example); and they attempt to examine or characterize education broadly. They may describe classroom experience and practice, but their goal is to address educational questions beyond simple descriptions of Steiner's ideas in practice. These questions changed from a seemingly simple first comprehensive English introduction to Steiner's ideas; through an Emersonian examination of fundamental questions of the meanings of education in the assumed context of the Cold War; and a re-casting of Waldorf education as an educational form that mirrors the growing counterculture and new age; to an indictment of misapplications of child psychology in education, for example. As the questions changed, a history emerged that shows Waldorf education changing in changing contexts. Waldorf education appears, then, not as a monolithic tablet on which the answers to an educational debate are inscribed, but as a partner in a dialogue. Admittedly, this partner has been increasingly silent in the United States over the past seventy years or so, but not necessarily less thoughtful or observant for that. Finally, even the term "Waldorf education" has its own history.

The Creation of Waldorf Education

History shows that even the term "Waldorf education," well accepted today, came into being only gradually. Interestingly, A. C. Harwood's title and index do not contain the word "Waldorf"; he does not use the phrase "Waldorf education" at all; and he refers only infrequently to "Waldorf schools," and then only as representing or modeling the "educational work" or "philosophy" of Rudolf Steiner. I enclose the term philosophy in quotation marks because of my conviction that Steiner's work does not constitute primarily a philosophy, but a methodology. Steiner deals with epistemological and ontological questions (see especially *Philosophy of Freedom* 1970), but his primary concern is the attainment of knowledge, not that knowledge itself; and a description of being, not a theory of it. More to the point here, his educational work is a work primarily in method.

John Gardner does not examine this point explicitly, but he does refer primarily to Steiner's "educational method." He refers to Waldorf schools and Waldorf education only in the central essay of the book, "The Experience of Knowledge," the single essay in which he is at pains to view Waldorf schools as models for the implementations of Steiner's method. The connotation here, different from the present, is that Steiner's method is not synonymous with the existence of education or schools that call themselves "Waldorf." In the "Foreword to the Second Edition" (1996), Gardner himself employs the word "Waldorf" in quotation marks. "I believe strongly in the excellence and soundness of the new insights that stand behind the Waldorf impulse in education; but I am less than enthusiastic about accepting the name generally used to designate this impulse, for it gives no clue as to what the new beginning actually intends or involves," he continues (12-13). Gardner would likely have agreed that any teacher and any school could, with good will, employ the model we have come to know as Waldorf education. (Compare Emmet, B. [undated] *From Farm to School: The Founding of the High Mowing School*).

M. C. Richards objectifies Waldorf education far more than these first two authors do. She refers to "Rudolf Steiner Education," "Waldorf Education," and "Waldorf schooling" interchangeably. Her tacit assumption (one that she represents in her generation, the Alternatives) is that Waldorf education, the curriculum, principles and practices of Waldorf schools, based on the work of Rudolf Steiner, possess a kind of concrete reality; that assumption is missing from the considerations of earlier authors. The subtle irony here is that her commitment to "become undivisive [sic] in our science, our emotions, our creativity—to live in the paradox of separateness and connection..." (156) is initially undermined by her acceptance of the objective existence of something called Waldorf education.

By 1999, Eugene Schwartz's index contains the following entries: Waldorf approach, Waldorf education, Waldorf high school, Waldorf kindergarten, Waldorf kindergarten playground, Waldorf main lesson, Waldorf method, Waldorf nursery teachers, Waldorf Room [sic], Waldorf school pupils, Waldorf schools, and Waldorf teachers. The process of objectification, clearly, does not end with the creation of one object, but threatens to continue indefinitely. Continued *ad absurdam*, the process would produce a "separate but equal" parallel "Waldorf" universe. Collecting them as I stumble across them, I have documented 51 uses of "Waldorf" as a qualifier:

Waldorf administrator
Waldorf advocate
Waldorf alliance
Waldorf alumni
Waldorf answer
Waldorf approach
Waldorf art(work)
Waldorf child(ren)
Waldorf crayon
Waldorf critic(ism)
Waldorf curriculum
Waldorf development
Waldorf doll
Waldorf education
Waldorf emphasis
Waldorf family
Waldorf festival
Waldorf fundraising
Waldorf furniture
Waldorf grace
Waldorf graduate
Waldorf history
Waldorf home
Waldorf homeschooling
Waldorf initiative
Waldorf inspired
Waldorf kindergarten
Waldorf library
Waldorf life skills
Waldorf math

Waldorf method
Waldorf movement
Waldorf music
Waldorf mythology
Waldorf orientation
Waldorf painting
Waldorf parent
Waldorf pedagogy
Waldorf philosophy
Waldorf prayer
Waldorf pupil
Waldorf resource
Waldorf ritual
Waldorf room
Waldorf school
Waldorf science
Waldorf student
Waldorf treasure
Waldorf trustee
Waldorf point of view
Waldorf world

Schwartz, of course, is not responsible for this onslaught of terminology; his vocabulary is simply the one that represents his generation, and the points he examines concern other aspects of education.

The objectification of Waldorf education is not an inherently reprehensible process. It eases discussion of important issues in education and creates a core around which communities of teachers, students, parents, and others may form. Although I raise the issue here, I have also relied on the term throughout this work. On the other hand, carried too far, objectification threatens to dichotomize an idea that, at least initially, opposed such a split. Discussion of Waldorf education, once created as an object, then poses itself "against" other forms of education, forms that must themselves be objectified even to be allowed into the discussion. Further, communities gathered around such an unquestioned, objectified idea may become insular. This process traces the rise of a fundamentalism to which Waldorf communities are certainly not immune. In a small way, the separation of "Waldorf" ideas about teaching and learning from more conventional or accepted ideas mirrors, for example, the separation of Protestantism from Catholicism in sixteenth-century Europe.

I have traced this process of objectification briefly with reference to a few books, but these are simply symptomatic of a wider process. The creation of the Association of Waldorf Schools of North America (AWSNA), also exemplifies this process. The Association began with informal conferences of about a dozen Waldorf schools in the mid-1960s and continued through a formal incorporation around 1980. Since then, the Association has obtained a service mark for use of the name "Waldorf" as it applies to education in the United States; categorized schools by affiliation status; decided that public schools cannot be Waldorf schools; and, most recently, become an accrediting body for Waldorf schools. This gradual institutionalization, necessary or helpful as it may have been to those involved, also charts the development of an exclusive educational precipitate, "Waldorf schools."

As Waldorf education became more established in the United States, its promise as a model for education generally was compromised, in part, by its objectification. By coming to reside, or to be seen to reside, in specific schools only, it forsook its status as a way to discuss how teachers teach and children learn, and became much more than that: an exclusive culture, ideology, and institution. This process may be traced through the books that I will now examine in more detail.

Before I proceed to the books themselves, however, I should point out three things. First, although the Steiner School in New York City opened in 1928, I am unaware of any book-length considered descriptive works in English on Waldorf education (excluding translations of Steiner's works) before Edmunds's of 1947 and Harwood's of 1958. This may reflect two characteristics of early practice: a thorough engagement with Steiner's work itself, especially including the translation of German material into English; and an active struggle in the few small schools and classrooms to survive from day to day and year to year, a struggle that left little time or energy for book-length reflections.

Second, especially because each of the books I will examine is born of experience, not of such activities as academic theorizing, agenda-setting, or policy-making, each book represents a culmination of life in a school or of thinking about education. For example, John Gardner's book was published in 1975, the year he retired after twenty-five years as faculty chair of the Waldorf School of Garden City. It is not a state-of-the-art examination, but a reflection of roughly the years 1950–1975. This point may seem obvious, but it points to the value of the books I will examine as historical artifacts. Each is a "summing up" of years prior to publication.

Third, although each successive author almost definitely knew of those preceding him or her, the later of these works contain few references to the earlier books (M. C. Richards refers readers to Harwood's book once, and Eugene Schwartz acknowledges a couple of contributions from John Gardner, but they seem to refer to personal conversations and not to published work.) This is odd given the very few works that aim at any sort of general description of Waldorf education, but may be understandable given the changing needs for a general work. Rather than sources or influences (or opportunities for rebuttal), previous works may simply be so much ink under the printing press, so to speak.

The Recovery of Man in Childhood

The Recovery of Man in Childhood, the first comprehensive attempt to summarize Rudolf Steiner's educational ideas for English speakers, enjoys the advantage of the first-born; it has no one to refute or imitate. The book, consequently, is a straightforward account that begins, after two thoughtful introductory chapters, with early childhood; and ends abruptly with the curriculum of the twelfth grade. Harwood was English, and a friend of C. S. Lewis, Owen Barfield, and J. R. R. Tolkein; and, with them, a member of "The Inklings." His book was published first in England but was imported immediately to the United States. The Myrin Institute, then in New York City, supported Harwood in writing the book, and the Institute then held the copyright (1958; revised ed. 2001). The book is dedicated, in fact, "to my very good friend H. A. W. M.," that is, to Alarik Myrin. Myrin, the Swedish-born American industrialist, you will recall, assisted with the founding of two Waldorf schools in the United States, the Waldorf Demonstration School of Adelphi College (later of Garden City), NY, and the Kimberton Farm School, PA (see Winkler 1970).

With Francis Edmunds, Stewart Easton, and others, Harwood represents a broad generation of English and Scottish Waldorf teachers and anthroposophists who lectured, taught, and even settled in the United States. With a contemporaneous group of mostly German speakers, they helped to transplant Steiner's ideas to the United States. A corollary group of Americans, including Henry Barnes, longtime faculty chair at the Rudolf Steiner School in New York City, traveled to England, Germany, and Switzerland to pursue an understanding of Steiner's work.

Separate from references to a sensibility somewhat more British than American; somewhat archaic language; and the general presumption that his audience is Christian; Harwood's book is relatively freer from historical consideration than are the other books I examine below. That is to say, it speaks more directly to longer-term questions of education and less to existing cultural or political contexts. Again, this is due in part to its status as first in the field; succeeding authors, although they do not necessarily acknowledge Harwood, are certainly aware of his work and must carve out a separate niche for themselves.

On the other hand, Harwood's central aim, the "marriage of the Arts and Sciences, a marriage in the core of their being, based on the ultimate unity of human experience…" (11). echoes an educational debate of the 1950s, at least, as it also reflects a longer-term Romantic interest in similar questions (see Barfield 1966). This post-war debate has been characterized, for example, briefly, well, and somewhat controversially, by Alston Chase (2000) with regard to Ted Kaszinski's (the Unabomber's) Harvard education; an education in Chase's view that sought to sunder the search for meaning in the humanities from truth obtained by science. This schism, and the search for a reconciliation of the humanities and natural science, outlined also in Barfield's lectures published as *History, Guilt, and Habit* (1979), underlies any true understanding of the goals of anthroposophy and Waldorf education.

As a summary of longer works by Rudolf Steiner and of long personal experience, Harwood's descriptions often threaten to collapse into stereotypes. Here Americans may read a British mind: "The inwardness of the girls [in adolescence] may easily degenerate into the horrors of backbiting and spitefulness; the externalism of the boys into the frightfulness of bullying and organized cruelty" (173). True, perhaps, but easier to imagine there and then. Each teacher and each generation must recast conceptions of, for example, adolescence, if they are not to miss contextual and cultural changes.

Harwood's writing is scarcely objectionable, but assumes his reader to be almost certainly a Christian. The last sentences of the book (1958 edition) provide an example. "The body is a House and a Temple, and it is the source and fountain of all forms and proportions. It is a secret known to the Christian religion in especial. To live in the body as in a Temple—this is the ultimate gift with which a Waldorf School would wish to send its children into the world" (208). (Perhaps taken with the German origins of their studies, many writers in English on Waldorf education adopt a style that involves more capitalization than is necessary.) Why Pantheists or Jews, for example, would have less claim to this idea than Christians is unclear.

The Experience of Knowledge

The Experience of Knowledge is a collection of John Gardner's essays, written over his twenty-five year tenure as faculty chairman of the Waldorf School of Garden City (originally the Waldorf Demonstration School of Adelphi College, an experimental school started largely at the behest of Adelphi trustee Alarik Myrin; it obtained autonomy from Adelphi in 1973 and incorporated a board of trustees in 1979). The book is organized in three parts. The first contains Gardner's earlier, philosophical essays on education. An example is "What is Man?" an essay that argues that human beings are more than "organisms," despite the reductive conclusions of John Dewey, Gestalt psychologists, and, especially, a now forgotten book, *Education and the Nature of Man* (Kelly and Rasey 1952). Gardner's central point is that self-knowledge, the springboard for any claims about the organismic (or other) nature of a human being, transcends necessarily the level of the organism alone. It necessitates recognition of an ego, and, hence, a moral stance.

Ego, self, or "I" in English are translated from *das Ich* in Steiner's German, not *das Ego*, and denote a concept difficult to translate. Steiner's notion of self implies a sort of essential and continuing individuality without the abstract connotations of a "thing" that cannot be divided; a self without necessarily implying selfishness or a changeable personality;

and an ego in a sense not freighted with Freudian or other psychoanalytic overtones. Some English authors have translated the concept as the "I," which works in print but is monumentally confusing when spoken because of the homonym "eye."

Gardner's argument here mirrors Steiner's discussion of "ethical individualism" (Steiner 1970) in seeing individualism not as a reduction from a social whole, nor as a manifestation of selfishness, but as the possibility of individual moral imagination and moral choice; choice that may in fact frequently contradict the impositions of "natural" drives and desires.

Part Two of Gardner's book addresses educational questions of intellect, truth, knowledge, experience, and morality. Unlike other essays, in which the philosophical discussion resists touching the ground, Gardner aims here to use the methods of education found in Waldorf schools to illustrate his points. He shows how truth, conceptualized in maturity as intellectual or logical truth, grows first through the activity (especially physical activity) of very young children, and then through the feelings and imaginations of elementary school-age children.

Without experiences of truth as action and without a feeling for truth, Gardner argues, we will be unlikely as adults to recognize it even intellectually. This three-stage description, based on Steiner's work and Gardner's observations, finds a clear parallel in Piaget's stages of the development of reasoning, his study of genetic epistemology. The term "sensori-motor" accords well with the experience of physical activity that Gardner describes; and Piaget's stage of "concrete operations" also parallels the manipulation of artistic materials that Waldorf teachers find so valuable in the elementary school.

On the other hand, although Piaget was an exacting researcher, his narrow focus neglects, perhaps, the *value* of behavior and affect, to favor the development of cognition. It is worth noting that some American educators have attached ages to Piaget's stages, something that he himself resisted (See, for example, Crain 1992, 122-134; and Piaget 1965.) That is, we could say that Piaget was interested in a precise description of the development of thinking, while some later authors have been interested in an educational application of Piaget's ideas. These latter have therefore quantified and simplified Piaget's work unnecessarily. That Steiner's rough seven-year periods of development do not accord exactly with Piaget's descriptions hardly matters; the point is that both are describing similar developmental processes; processes that are cumulative, integrative, and metamorphic. That is, development for both Steiner and Piaget involves "sea changes," not ladder-like accumulations or accretions.

The title essay of Gardner's book resides in this central section, and it offers Gardner's only introduction to the educational methods of Waldorf schools. Gardner emphasizes, for example, "the cognitive power that lies hidden in feeling and will" (66). He discovers in the cognitive act of learning to read, for example, the necessity for "a vivid experience of the creative, formative powers that lie within language" (67). We might say that the method used to teach reading hardly matters (whole language versus phonics, for example) if a child's imagination and interest are not engaged. Although this reads like a truism, the sterility of "Dick and Jane" readers points to neglect of this necessity, at least earlier in the twentieth century.

For a historical consideration of Gardner's book, the third part is the most instructive. The essays here are mature reflections of "problems of special interest to parents and citizens" (v). The essays hew closely to accepted broad principles of Waldorf education in that they are concerned with inspiring genius, developing the possibility of individual freedom, and separating schools from government control, as goals for education.

The essays also reflect, particularly and often deliberately, concerns of many Americans who perceived political and cultural threats to democracy, individualism and freedom, however conceived, during the Cold War. That is, they stand in clear opposition to, at least, stereotypical conceptions of the threats of Marxist-Leninist socialism: political totalitarianism, cultural indoctrination, and economic communism. Gardner's arguments are not arguments from the right, however; at least not in the conventional sense. They recognize, for example, that philosophical materialism may underlie both capitalism and communism; and that the Soviet Union and China are not the only nations that might seek to indoctrinate rather than educate their students. In this sense, Gardner's arguments aim to transcend the Cold War deadlock, while acknowledging it as the foundation of a discourse. In this aim it is surprisingly similar, for example, to that of Aleksander Solzhenitsyn's commencement address at Harvard University in 1978. Both Gardner and Solzhenitsyn see a solution to the political and economic standoff of the times in individual transformation. To apply their concerns to later issues: the world may cheer the fall of the Berlin Wall and the dissolution of the Soviet Union, but tensions remain between social responsibility and individual freedom; and between reductive materialism and a qualitative, synthetic understanding of the world.

If Gardner's arguments ring of Emersonian transcendentalism, it is no accident. Gardner taught transcendentalist literature for years; published several lectures on transcendental writers; and clearly strove, within the form of the essay, for an Emersonian economy of words. His success in this regard was not complete; not that it could be. He titled one essay "Authority, Discipline, and Freedom"; that would have been at least three essays for Emerson, had he wished to tackle subjects so abstract. Gardener's begins, "Those who dispute about how to educate free men argue the effects of childish obedience upon adult self-reliance; of unquestioning trust and belief in authority during the first school years upon the critical thinking that enables a mature individual later on to steer his way past illusion" (117). Emerson's vocabulary and locutions aside, Gardner sets up a debate between Cold War straw men and proceeds to demonstrate how each is only partially correct (and neither is mutually exclusive). Such rhetoric falls short of Emerson's direct and pithy expression.

On the other hand, in his interest in Emerson (three of ten essays begin by quoting Emerson), Gardner forwards a previous theme of my research, the notion that Waldorf education, taken not as an object but as an expression of a method, derives from influences that predate Steiner. Chief among them for Americans is Emerson.

A second edition of Gardner's book was published in 1996 under the title *Education in Search of Spirit*. Despite a note that the new edition has been "revised, updated, and expanded," there are few changes. Some of these few changes, however, are noteworthy. In "Morality and the Experience of Knowledge," for example, Gardner originally had written, "The self *will* out [of its solitary confinement]. Drugs, sex, speed, civil disobedience, and revolution seem to offer ways out; but the trouble with all of them is that their ways are illusory" (97). In 1996, the same passage reads, "Drugs, sex, speed, and rebellion seem to offer ways out…"

(111). Despite similarities, it is easy to read a polemic against the civil unrest of the late 1960s and early 1970s in the first quotation; and to catch a recognition of the possible virtues of civil disobedience and revolution in the second. The drama of the times is tempered in retrospect.

In a discussion of "the path of redemption [following the] Fall of Man," the second edition inserts the phrase, "…whose time must come and has come, if the Fall is not to be final" (173). Coupled with the following tortured, pessimistic observation, added to the new edition, we read, it seems, the personality change of the author, from active teacher to passive observer:

> As the Western world feels the helplessness of its own predominantly material, technological, economic orientation to master soul sickness and social distemper as these are appearing in depression, addictions, criminality, the dissolving of moral values, and the whole tide of destructive behavior afflicting millions of the younger generation— what is to prevent us from being drawn quite out of our orbit? (170)

The foreword to the second edition suggests that, even in Waldorf schools, head and hands suffer the neglect of heart. To remedy this perceived lack, Gardner suggests what he calls the "direct approach" to the spirit (or "Spirit"; several words are apocalyptically capitalized in the second edition), "intensified wonder, delight, and grateful praise… only spirit finds spirit. … Only the real Self can answer: 'I truly want…'" (14-15). These concepts, which suffer by comparison with the relative clarity of Gardner's earlier writing, I believe, accord more with Gardner's late interest in "charismatic Christianity" than they do with Steiner's work (See Gardner 1992). In his interests in transcendentalism, the Cold War, and, later, fundamentalist Christianity, Gardner reflects concerns that accord well with the generation of Waldorf schools that I call "The Americans."

Toward Wholeness

If Gardner's voice aims at the prophetic and Emersonian, M. C. Richards' voice in *Toward Wholeness: Rudolf Steiner Education in America* aims at the oracular. "In new age consciousness, the religious impulse continues to evolve. Like the sun, it shines across all divisions" (156). As with many, many pronouncements in Richards' book, we may agree or disagree; but we are given little to support a discussion. This is not to say that Richards does not present a progression from idea to idea, but that the ideas are too often ill-examined or axiomatic. What exactly are "new age consciousness" and "the religious impulse"?

Another example demonstrates the limits of her approach. Richards teases apart Steiner's concept of *Geisteswissenschaft*, translated literally as "spiritual science." This word normally describes what in English speaking countries are the studies called the humanities or human sciences; but Steiner intended to revive, in part, its older meaning as a knowledge of the human being conceived as microcosmic mirror of the macrocosmic universe (See, for example, Hildegard of Bingen, quoted in Fox 1987) and as a being of body, soul, and spirit.

"Spiritual science," Richards writes, is science that is "not a tool... not intellectual science." Well, natural science is not necessarily a tool, either. And spiritual science may be more than merely intellectual science; but it is certainly intellectual, too. She says both too much and too little in the same sentence. "Spirit uses intellect but goes beyond it. Spiritual science requires the union of inner perception (spiritual) and objectivity (science)" (43). The spiritual may involve "inner perception," although Richards would agree there's much more to it than this; but objectivity, while scientific, is also spiritual. In fact, Steiner' spiritual science aims to overcome the apparent dichotomy between objective and subjective experience; not in blending or coupling them, nor in using one to destroy the other; but in transcending them—or, equally, discovering the immanence of one in the presence of the other—to discover a common source for each. Semantically, of course, the term "subjective" implies both its opposite, "objective," and a pair of negations, "non-subjective" and "non-objective." But this semiotic-rectangular view of these concepts is reductive and analytical. A synthetic view, which, like a geometric proof, can be obtained only through an intuitive, participatory leap, and not through an explanation, discovers the situational or contextual unity of experience. "Subjective" and "objective" do not cancel each other out in meaninglessness; they are poles between which experience is lived.

In searching for an analogy or example to describe this unity of experience, Richards employs "the [physicist's] recognition that the observer is part of the observed." This principle contradicts our naïve understanding of cause and effect, but does not reach what might better be called the unity of quantity and quality. The indeterminacy—and apparent unity—of the principles of physics does not lead to understanding or to love.

Richards' book reads like a collection of essays. But for a few introductory chapters and a conclusion, the contents leap around, from "Education as an Art" to "Teacher Training and Handwork" (in itself an odd combination, understandable in view of Richards' work as a potter and educator). In its deliberate embrace of the "new age" and its view of Steiner's work as "alternative," it represents the generation of schools I call "The Alternatives."

Millennial Child

The three strongest complementary and intertwined themes of *Millennial Child* are these: that education at the turn of the millennium should address, above all, children's will; that education should increasingly concern itself with young (preschool and elementary age) children; and that Waldorf education offers the most appropriate curriculum or pedagogy with which to address these children.

To argue these points, Eugene Schwartz constructs an interpretation of history in which literacy, promoted first in Europe by Charlemagne, grows through the middle ages to the founding of the first universities. The general path since then for European culture, Schwartz argues, has been for educators to concern themselves with increasingly younger children. We have seen the rise and decline of the present conventional curriculum of the "three Rs," Schwartz says; and the Waldorf curriculum, broadly conceived, is "the" curriculum, now in its infancy, that will grow to become the new tradition or convention. Following Rudolf Steiner's picture of child development, this increasing concern with the education of young children winds its way down from the intellectual concerns of university and, later, high school students through a concern with the emotions, feelings, and imagination of older elementary school students, to Schwartz's present concern with the will-education of young children.

It is interesting to note here, as Joan Almon (1999), has pointed out, that the original Waldorf School in Stuttgart had a kindergarten for approximately half of one school year during Steiner's lifetime. It was run by Elizabeth Grunelius, who later worked at several schools in the United States. Steiner's education lectures generally concern children age seven and older, although he did speak extensively about child development during the first seven years of life. The point is that much of the preschool curriculum in Waldorf schools has been worked out and implemented since Steiner's death.

In tracing this history, Schwartz relies on an interpretation of history that sees decades, centuries, and millennia divided into thirds. Further, in his scheme, the first third of each period concerns particularly thinking, the second third concerns feeling, and the last third, will. Given this picture, the change to the present millennium sees a triple-threat in the realm of will: the end of a decade, a century, and a millennium. Schwartz's argument is strongest with regard to generations of approximately 33 years each. Historians, whether they subscribe to them or not, are almost universally familiar with interpretations according to generations. Our decade-obsessed and label-conscious twentieth and twenty-first centuries seem especially open to arguments based on generations. Less familiar are Schwartz's divisions of century and millennium, and readers will have to validate Schwartz's claims here according to their own experience. I am unfamiliar with such arguments, and can find little basis to substantiate them in Steiner's work; but I am unwilling to dismiss them out of hand. If there are esoteric sources for these ideas, Schwartz has not cited them.

Schwartz's most significant example of his historical structure is the metamorphosis of Freud's thought in the first third of the twentieth century into feeling (particularly as expressed in the work of Dr. Spock, a closet Freudian) in the middle of the century; and finding expression in the will in the last part of the century. I find myself arguing, however, that the thought of the behaviorists in the first third of the century (and after); of Piaget in the middle third (and after); and of systems theorists in the last third, each greatly intellectual; have had at least as much influence in education as has the thought of Freud, especially outside the Northeastern United States.

Further, Schwartz finds powerful evidence for the necessity of a will-oriented education in the spate of diagnoses of Attention Deficit Hyperactivity Disorder (ADHD), characterized by "overactivity, restlessness, distractibility, and short attention span, especially in young children." In short, ADHD represents the social and historical problem of "uncontrolled will." Schwartz traces the rise of ADHD and the disorders from which it grew ("minimal brain dysfunction" and "hyperkinetic reactions of childhood)"over the past thirty years or so. He clearly lays out diagnoses and treatments based on perceived chemical, emotional, and behavioral causes. By adding a fourth category, "multiple causes," which must be addressed holistically and phenomenologically, Schwartz recognizes an ego disorder (as opposed to the physical, etheric, or astral disorders implied by previous causes).

His discussion, however, may not go far enough. He skates around the clear possibility that ADHD is culturally produced. Here Freud's work offers an excellent meta-example: he made his reputation in Vienna treating women suffering from "hysterical paralysis," a psychological disease produced by upper-middle-class culture in Vienna in the late 1800s. The symptoms (usually paralysis of the hands and forearms) were real and debilitating; but they, and their diagnosis and treatment, disappeared with changed roles for women in society shortly after the turn of the century. The point is that ADHD is likely a similar malady. Plop enough kids in front of various phosphorescent screens long enough, at home and at school; feed them on Fritos and water them on caffeinated soda; remove them from meaningful participation in family and community life and they'll likely deserve an ADHD diagnosis. As the eminent developmental psychologist Howard Gruber says, "The schools have ADHD, not the kids." And we might add, also the homes, restaurants, playgrounds, and day-care centers. Strong evidence for this claim lies in the fact that ADHD affects boys, primarily (just as anorexia nervosa and bulimia affect girls, primarily). Teachers and therapists obviously have to deal with what confronts them, but to argue for treatment of symptoms (even with the most anthroposophic, phenomenological, holistic approach) without addressing the larger cultural and social context, points education once again in the dangerous direction of asking teachers to solve society's ills (see Traub 2000).

A final concern is that Steiner's words about education and child development regard fully the first twenty-one years or so of life. If we must adopt the language of crisis in discussing education, then that crisis cuts across all ages. The will education of young children, at home and in school, matures potentially into freedom; but the education of adolescents in love and intellect matures potentially into true regard for universal brotherhood, according to Steiner. Is it possible to say that one is more important today than another? Schwartz's good assumption is that ADHD, teen violence, and other modern maladies of adolescence are better addressed years, not days, before they manifest themselves. Schwartz pursues his discussion with virtually no reference, however, to high school-age children. "Waldorf education" in *Millennial Child* must be translated as "Waldorf education up to the age of about fourteen." Readers first encountering Waldorf education in these pages (and Schwartz's intended audience, it seems, is primarily one that has an interest in, but little familiarity with, Waldorf education) will find it difficult to conceive of a Waldorf high school education at all. In this, *Millennial Child* propagates a truncated view of Waldorf education.

Toward the end of *Millennial Child*, Schwartz quotes Steiner: "The Waldorf School is not an 'alternative' school like so many others founded in the belief that they will correct all the errors of one kind or another in education. It is founded on the idea that the best principles and the best will in this field can come into effect only if the teacher understands human nature." Some mainstream educators may well accept Schwartz's assertion that the time is ripe for a new, appropriately post-Renaissance, post-Enlightenment, even post-Modern educational form. The recurring arguments, experiments, and crises in education in the last century or so are possibly the death throes of the school of the past. The force of Schwartz's argument, however, lies not in the prescription of the brand "Waldorf education," at which many educators would rightly take offence; but in the recognition of the historical, social, and individual necessity for an education, of whatever name, which is based on the wisdom of humanity. In its attempt to re-engage in a conversation with educators outside the circle of Waldorf schools; and in its re-interpretation of Waldorf education to address immediate social concerns (ADHD), Schwartz's book represents the generation of schools that I call "The Social Missionaries."

Fidelity and Flexibility

A fifth book is Ida Oberman's fascinating and much-needed historical study of Waldorf education in Germany and the United States, *Fidelity and Flexibility in Waldorf Education*, 1919–1998. It supports my division of the history of Waldorf schools into generations, representing three of them in its third section. Oberman's book is divided into three sections. The first examines the first Waldorf School in Stuttgart from its founding until Rudolf Steiner's death in 1925. The second examines the course of Waldorf education in Germany after Steiner's death, and during the rise and reign of the Nazis. The third traces the transplantation of Waldorf education to the United States.

The first section locates the origin of the first Waldorf school in Steiner's intellectual biography. From his interests in Goethe and theosophy; through the founding of the Anthroposophical Society; to the threefold social movement, Oberman details the bases for a curriculum based in German cultural history; school administration independent of the state ("free" schooling); and the idea of schooling as social transformation. By anchoring the founding of the first school in the realities of Steiner's life, and in the social and political life of Germany after World War I, Oberman provides perspective on what otherwise can seem like a Waldorf Decalogue, handed down once and for all without apparent compromise or context. To add to the context or "cultural field" described by Oberman, as Nancy Parsons Whittaker has suggested, the curriculum of the first school, for example, was also constrained by state requirements and by the strengths and weaknesses of those whom Steiner recommended as teachers.

In the second section, Oberman locates a structure for understanding the history of the spread of Waldorf schools in the actions and reactions of anthroposophists and Waldorf teachers upon Steiner's death. Some, like Marie Steiner, strove to preserve in purity their understanding of Steiner's wishes. Others, like Hermann von Baravalle, sought to accommodate their understanding of Waldorf education and anthroposophy to their understanding of their audience. And still others, like Ita Wegman, tried to further an understanding of Steiner's indications through a process of evolution.

Oberman then examines the activity of German Waldorf schools during the rise to power of the Nazis. Her findings, carefully and sensitively presented, should really be no surprise. Too often we forget the ease with which we read history backward, knowing the results, forgetting that this is a luxury denied to those who lived through it. That some parents and Waldorf teachers saw parallels between Nazi ideology and the German culture as presented in Waldorf school curricula should not surprise us. Neither should the fact that some teachers argued for making compromises with the state in order to keep schools open as long as possible. Nor should the subtle resistance of Waldorf teachers who discovered a radio "broken" just at the time students were required to listen to a broadcast by Hitler. Nor should Oberman's description of Hitler's picture (display required by law) side by side with Steiner's on a school wall. These details and many others provide a vivid picture of teachers, parents, and students living through turmoil central to the twentieth century.

Turning her attention to the United States, Oberman finds the strategies or modes of operation that arose following Steiner's death—purity, accommodation, and evolution—in U.S. Waldorf schools. She describes the first school, the Rudolf Steiner School of New York City, as one that pursued a "quest for purity" by hiring a number of native German speakers familiar with Waldorf education, and by hewing closely to the curriculum of the original school in Stuttgart. Further, with the closing of Waldorf schools in Germany, Oberman describes the New York school as assuming the mantle of leadership among Waldorf schools. Whether or not other schools internationally accepted this decision (or even knew of it), is another matter. Oberman's description of the New York school as one seeking purity is generally accurate, I believe. Curative or therapeutic eurythmy was called *Heil* eurythmy throughout the 1930s, and the school reported annually not only to "Headquarters" (the New York City Anthroposophical branch office), but also to Stuttgart. On the other hand, Hermann von Baravalle, Oberman's accommodationist, lectured to the faculty and community frequently, and was offered the position of director of the school in the late 1930s. He refused, for reasons of his own. Faculty meeting minutes also reveal that a debate occurred as to whether or not it was appropriate for teachers in American Waldorf schools to have German (or other) accents. Such examples are numerous. Purity, to the extent it was sought by the New York school, was not sought without contest.

More importantly, it seems clear that any school founded at this time (there was, in the United States, only this one, so we have no basis for comparison) would be founded along the lines of Oberman's search for purity. The times, the generation, offer little else, just as later times and later generations would not tolerate such an attempt to import Waldorf education pure and unchanged.

Oberman describes the constellation of people around the founding of the Kimberton, Pennsylvania, school, von Baravalle and Alarik Myrin chief among them, as a group that sought to minimize the anthroposophic ground from which Waldorf education grew. Here again, Oberman is largely correct, I believe. I have greater familiarity with the Garden City, New York, school, Myrin's second school; and the history of this school also speaks to an attempt to accommodate what the founders saw as a more pragmatic American attitude, one that had little interest in promoting anthroposophy to parents or a larger community. (Rather, especially through the Myrin Institute for Adult Education, they sought to promote fruitful ideas that were often, but not always, grounded in anthroposophy, without discussing anthroposophy itself publicly.) Von Baravalle and Elizabeth Grunelius, both teachers in the first school in Stuttgart, were present in the very early years of the Garden City school, but soon left the school to the Americans.

Despite my admiration for and agreement with most of what Oberman writes, I take exception to two particulars. The first is her use of the unqualified "Waldorf" to mean Waldorf education, ideology, and reform. It is a convenient shorthand, as in the phrases, "how Waldorf followers use the past in their present," or "the history of Waldorf in America." On the other hand, it reifies and objectifies a form of education that only gradually came to be so calcified after seventy or more years of history. It is a historical weakness, then, that the careful reader must guard against; especially, for example, when it is inserted unwarranted into a quotation from Emil Molt and Fritz von Bothmer: "The faculty now active at this school have proven... their willingness to continue this [Waldorf] work..." That they did *not* call it "Waldorf" work is a historical fact, indicative of a less exclusive point of view, one that deserves greater recognition.

Second, Oberman represents Waldorf education, primarily through its schools, as an "ideology" and a "German reform." Oberman refers to Steiner's "target group," for example, and to Waldorf education's "theater of expansion." No doubt historical actors have treated Waldorf education as an ideology operating to reform in a theater of expansion.

One should also include, however, consideration for the ways in which Waldorf education strives not to be ideological, and does not necessarily represent a German reform; or a "reform" of any but the most expansive, inclusive kind. Reform implies an activist agenda, and plenty of Waldorf teachers have been and are activists. An understanding of freedom or of Waldorf education, however, does not particularly support (or deny support for) any but the most personally transformative activism. And from another point of view, Waldorf schools have resisted expansion, cloistering themselves, spending most of a century perfecting an exclusive jargon. This is part of their history, too.

Conclusion

Through the work of Harwood, Gardner, Richards, Schwartz, and Oberman, we can trace, on the one hand, the precipitation of the concept "Waldorf" out of the work of Rudolf Steiner and into its employment in the United States. On the other hand, we can trace a fluid discourse that defines or describes Waldorf education in terms that necessarily take into account historical and cultural contexts. Both processes have proceeded largely unconsciously. For each author, that is, the contemporaneous concept of "Waldorf education" is little in question, except as it opposes or addresses some question of education generally. Similarly, for each author, historical context is seen not so much as a temporary or contingent situation, but as the given ground for argument. As contexts change, therefore, these representative books become relatively obsolete, rocks in a river of change, and anyone seeking to know Waldorf education in the present must seek largely elsewhere.

6. WALDORF SCHOOLS TODAY, WALDORF SCHOOLS TOMORROW

LAWRENCE CREMIN, then professor of history and education at Teachers College, New York City, spoke at the 50th anniversary celebration of the Rudolf Steiner School in New York, held in Milbank Chapel at Teachers College in 1978. His remarks were not recorded or published, but their gist, recalled by Douglas Sloan, was this: alternative movements in education in the United States live briefly, contribute their small part to the mainstream, and then dissolve and disappear. Steiner or Waldorf education is such an alternative movement and will, almost inevitably, follow this route (Personal communication 1997).

The history of Waldorf education in the United States so far, however, counters this statement. The growth of Waldorf schools over the past decades years, from 1928 to the present, has been roughly exponential, at least until recently, and, perhaps more impressive, the forms that Waldorf education has taken, especially within the past twenty years, although increasingly diverse, are as yet undiluted.

How Many Waldorf Schools are There?

It is more difficult than you might suppose to say how many Waldorf schools there are in the United States. This is true even if you count only schools affiliated with the Association of Waldorf Schools of North America (AWSNA), which holds a federal service mark on the use of the name "Waldorf" with regard to education in the United States. According to AWSNA, only independent (what are colloquially called "private") schools can be Waldorf schools; and AWSNA lists 120 such schools as of this writing in the spring of 2011.

AWSNA also lists ninety "WECAN" (Waldorf Early Childhood Association of North America) schools, however; many of these overlap with schools listed on the main AWSNA list. Of these ninety, however, one is actually in Canada, and one school is listed twice—so the number here is eighty-eight.

Further, WECAN has its own list on its own website, and lists 147 programs. Some of these are child care or parent-toddler programs; and therefore it seems they aren't counted elsewhere as schools.

Correlating the AWSNA and WECAN lists we come close to the actual number of independent educational programs and schools that use educational methods derived from the work of Rudolf Steiner. We may count 224 distinct early childhood programs; more than half of these are connected with independent Waldorf schools that also have at least elementary grades. There are approximately ninety-six independent programs, some with high schools as well, that educate children through eighth grade; and there are approximately thirty-four Waldorf high schools. Some of these are "stand alone" high schools, like the Tara Performing Arts High School in Boulder, Colorado; or the High Mowing School in Wilton, New Hampshire; but most are extensions of existing elementary Waldorf schools. At least one, the Monadnock Waldorf High School in Keene, New Hampshire, is young enough that it does not, as of this writing, have all four high school grades.

I write "approximately" because some schools are listed without grade ranges, and because it is difficult to know if these lists are complete and up-to-date. What about small schools that are too young to use the name Waldorf, given AWSNA's trademark; schools that now meet in a rented church or even a donated living room; schools that may or may not survive and grow eventually to be counted by AWSNA? What about informal homeschool groups in which parents and teachers use Waldorf methods? What about Waldorf-trained teachers in public schools, who teach their classes using Steiner's methods without acknowledgment?

And what of schools that have closed—the Sunrise Farm School in the early 1940s, and others since? What is the failure rate for Waldorf schools? In 1999 there were ninety-one AWSNA-affiliated schools in the United States; in 2003 there were 111; and, in 2010, 134. Between 1999 and 2003, two schools (the International Waldorf School of Miami, Florida; and the Finger Lakes Waldorf School of Ithaca, New York) closed, a failure rate of less than 2 percent in four years. (Since then, the Ithaca school reorganized and re-opened, and at least one new school has been founded in Florida.) During this time, twenty-two additional schools had become affiliated with AWSNA. Of these, sixteen, or nearly 15 percent, existed prior to 1999, but were not on AWSNA's "radar" in that year. The remaining four schools were founded in 1999. (Two schools did not list founding dates.) Schools founded between 2000 and 2003 are clearly too young, then, to appear in a 2003 count. Judging from past numbers, however, it is safe to say that there may be two dozen or more schools that have already been founded but that are growing anonymously. Most of these will have been founded in the past three years or so, but several may have been founded significantly earlier.

Three schools are included in the 2003 count that do not appear in the 1999 count, and yet were founded before 1990. These are the Redmont School in South Birmingham, Alabama (1987); the Na Kamalei School, Kilauea, Hawaii (1983); and the Somerset School, Colfax, California (1978). The Somerset School "serves special needs children" (www.bobnancy.com, 2003), and likely existed as an independent non-Waldorf affiliated school before adopting Waldorf school methods. In order to appear in the AWSNA count, schools must have demonstrated viability (although the criteria for this are not clear), and be sponsored by or affiliated with an existing school. Depending on circumstances, this process can take anywhere from a few years to a couple of decades.

At least one existing school (the Wolakota Waldorf School, of Kyle, South Dakota, on the Pine Ridge Reservation) is not listed. Other independent initiatives that have yet to rise to the level of AWSNA affiliation, are likely "out there" but difficult to find and count.

Schools not affiliated with AWSNA, such as charter schools, may call themselves only "Waldorf inspired" or "Waldorf methods" schools, and they do not appear on the AWSNA website. A group of administrators on the West Coast has formed the Alliance for Public Waldorf Education (APWE), and maintains a database that currently includes forty-four public and charter schools that use Waldorf methods. Susan Olsen, administrator at the Sebastopol Independent Charter School, shared this database with me. She was clear, however, that this number might be too low. More charters are submitted and approved all the time, and the database necessarily lags a bit behind this growth.

Correlating all lists, private and public, we may say that there are currently at least 269 schools or programs, private or public, from early childhood through high school, based in Waldorf methods. Some of these are long-established schools with a full range of grades from early childhood through high school, with enrollments between 300 and 400 students. Others are little more than play groups for very young children.

How Many Waldorf Schools are There?

Estimating the number of children who receive education based in Waldorf methods is even harder than counting schools. If we grant that an average of all school enrollments might be 100 students, then we can say that there are between 25,000 and 30,000 Waldorf students in the United States, approximately one-third of them in charter or public schools (which tend to have larger average enrollments than private schools). According to Betty Staley and others, given that charter school growth is currently outpacing the growth of independent schools, there will soon be more students in Waldorf charter schools than there are in independent Waldorf schools.

There is currently some tension between AWSNA and APWE. This tension is difficult to comprehend fully, although I asked both public and independent Waldorf school teachers and administrators about it. An APWE representative told me that "the only three people in the United States who are still afraid of public Waldorf schools are in the leadership of AWSNA." This individual predicted that AWSNA would soon find itself "irrelevant," as public Waldorf schools grow in number and importance, and as independent Waldorf schools fail to keep pace with the professionalism, professional development, and accountability demanded of public schools. On the other hand, AWSNA representatives spoke of the "dishonesty" of some charter schools in representing themselves as being more steeped in Waldorf methods than they truly are, or in playing down their involvement with state politics and standards.

The number of Waldorf school students ignores those who are home-schooled using Waldorf methods; this is a number impossible to ascertain, but it is certainly growing as homeschooling grows. Arkansas and

Nebraska are among the nine states in which I could locate no Waldorf schools; they have vibrant homeschooling websites that include information on and resources relating to Waldorf homeschooling. Closer to home, I am aware of at least two informal homeschool groups constituted by parents who band together, register as homeschoolers, and then hire teachers without incorporating a school. How many such informal arrangements like this exist, and how they are growing, is impossible to say.

Even if we could count the number of students homeschooled, we would still omit those students in public schools who have former private school Waldorf teachers now teaching in public schools. Tom Roepke in New York City is educated in Waldorf methods and experienced in independent Waldorf school teaching. According to his peers in public school, when Roepke's students are particularly well behaved, Tom has "used his 'Waldorf' on them" as if it were a sort of educational martial art. Again, it is not possible to say how many such teachers and administrators there are, or how many students they have, or to what extent they are able to use Waldorf methods in their classrooms. As Steiner said, however, his method may be applied anywhere there is the will to use it.

If you touch a paintbrush loaded with yellow watercolor paint to a damp sheet of paper, as a young student in a Waldorf school might do, the paint, concentrated at the center, will spread, thinning and raying out. This fuzzy image is a metaphor for the attempt to count Waldorf schools and Waldorf students in the United States. Toward the center, it's clear what is a school and what is not; who is a Waldorf student and who is not. Toward the edges, however, the image is so diffuse that it becomes difficult to say where and when and how Steiner's methods are used, or who is educated according to them.

Distribution

Time-lapse photography over the past decades would show Waldorf schools spreading across the United States in perhaps a predictable fashion, flowing into the centers of money and influence; first the East Coast (New York, 1928); then the West Coast (Los Angeles, 1955); and then the Great Lakes (Detroit, 1965). Waldorf schooling moved into

Colorado (Denver, 1974) almost a decade later. In 1980, the first school in Texas opened (Austin). Two years later, the first school in Virginia opened (Crozet, near Charlottesville, 1982), followed by a slow creep south and west (Chapel Hill, 1984; Atlanta, 1986; Birmingham, 1987; St. Louis and Louisville, 1993.) There are at least five Waldorf schools in Hawaii, the oldest dating back to 1961; and a Waldorf school opened in Anchorage, Alaska, in 1992.

Growth

Intuition might have us believe that growth is arithmetic, that it proceeds by accumulation; but it more often proceeds geometrically, especially when it is organic. That is, like an epidemic, it involves a periodic doubling. At first, growth appears slow because the doubling from one to two and two to four has little absolute value. After five generations, however, the same rate of doubling causes thirty-two to become sixty-four; and sixty-four becomes one hundred twenty-eight. The numbers are larger, but the rate of growth is constant.

Growth in the number of Waldorf schools in the United States is geometric, mirroring closely a doubling every ten years. The growth of independent Waldorf schools appears to have slowed through the 1990s and the first decade of the 2000s, but if we include charter schools, the number of schools continues to increase at the same rate it has followed for decades. If we imagine that a finite but growing number of people set out to found Waldorf schools each decade, some of those in the 1990s and 2000s founded charter schools within public systems when they might in different circumstances have founded independent schools.

Patrice Maynard, for one, objects to claims that Waldorf school growth may be seen as doubling; instead, she claims a slow growth that accelerated rapidly in the 1980s, then decelerated again. A table she drew to illustrate her point, however, includes only AWSNA schools, and stretches the first decade from 1928 to 1940. It all depends on how you look at it, I suppose, and what you want to say with your data. Certainly, the geometric growth of schools is only an approximation.

If charter schools (and other public or unrecognized initiatives) are considered to be categorically different from conventional independent

Waldorf schools, then the growth curve for Waldorf schools is leveling off; the growth curve may be becoming sigmoid.

Several of those I interviewed or spoke with believe that, because an upturn in growth appears to coincide with the ascendancy of the counterculture in the late 1960s, a "new age" consciousness is somehow responsible for this growth. This may be the case; schools have grown not only in numbers, but also in enrollments; but frankly, it's too close to call. An "elbow" near 1970 seems more likely because of a lag through the sixties and an acceleration afterwards, if it has any significance at all. The numbers are too small here to have statistical significance, but the growth suggests the possibility that the turmoil of the sixties actually retarded the growth of schools somewhat, while the eighties saw growth that slightly out-paces previous rates.

Conservative Lives

Coloring the post-World War II generations, which include all but the first Waldorf school in the United States, are the remarkable prosperity and conservatism of the entire past half-century. The Civil Rights, women's, and environmental movements, despite acknowledged and important progress, may represent "tinkering" with an adequate system. (And perhaps it is tinkering that makes sense in a growing economy, bringing people of color and women to the job market.) They do not represent crises of a magnitude sufficient to reorder society, however, as did those surrounding the Civil War or the Great Depression. The martyrs and dissidents of the past forty years are important heroes; but for most Americans of any color or gender, the primary fact of life has been the prosperity and world dominance of American business and American mass culture. Waldorf schools presently enjoy a small niche as alternatives to more conventional education, both public and private. They have expanded within that niche; but why there are not a thousand Waldorf schools, or ten thousand? A large part of the answer, external to the culture of Waldorf schools themselves, may lie in the brute effects of prosperity. Comfort has placed a lid on social change.

My thesis here is hardly unique; and it may be seen, for example, as a corollary to Godfrey Hodgson's (1976) "liberal consensus" ("liberal" here refers to classical political and philosophical liberalism; that is, it posits individualism as the health of the state, and looks more like what Americans are used to calling conservatism than anything else). More recent historians recognize the same basic point:

> Despite the challenges of the 1960s, there remains an enormous commitment among most Americans to religion, the nuclear family, and powerful "old fashioned" ideas such as individualism, upward mobility, anti-Communism, and middle-class propriety. The persistence of these views, in turn, goes hand in hand with a relatively static distribution of political and economic resources. Notwithstanding changes in matters of race and gender, the basic alignment of classes in the United States is much as it was in 1940 and in recent years has become even more rigid. (Chafe 1990)

On the other hand, it is reasonable to ask why there are any Waldorf schools at all. There were approximately a dozen schools by 1970, and without the heroic efforts of many people, there might have been fewer, or none at all. For Waldorf schools to sustain their rate of growth, those first, pioneering schools had to survive in a climate generally unfriendly to European culture and alternative schooling. Other more famous educational experiments, like A. S. Niell's Summerhill, exist as anachronisms, not as part of a growing, world-wide educational movement.

Groups and Individuals

In writing this history, I have become increasingly aware that a large part of it rests on the shoulders of a few outstanding people, some of whom I've mentioned earlier. Hermann von Baravalle, for example, is associated with virtually all of the pre-1970 schools. He was an advisor to the Rudolf Steiner School in New York, where he was offered the directorship (he declined); a teacher at the High Mowing School; a founder of the Garden City school; a nationwide lecturer in cities that soon had Waldorf schools, including Chicago and Detroit; and a teacher at the Highland Hall School in Los Angeles. Without doubt, he is first among the Europeans.

Among the Americans, John Gardner and Henry Barnes stand out. Many Waldorf schools have distanced themselves from an administrative model that includes a strong leader, and John Gardner is often vilified for having been a "headmaster." On the other hand, many established schools have teachers who were trained by Mr. Gardner in Garden City at Adelphi University before 1979, when his institute was forced to close.

One of the reasons I mention these individuals is that there is a tendency among Waldorf teachers to say, in essence, "Back in the old days, rich anthroposophists could start a school single-handedly, even if no one wanted it." Or, "Someone like John Gardner could be a charismatic leader, but we don't go for that anymore. Now we do everything by consensus and the impulse for new schools comes from parents." These ideas are usually not expressed as characterizing historical differences, but as rhetoric to say that the new way is better and truer to the original aims of Waldorf education; and the old days were misguided and authoritarian.

In general, there has been confusion over some historical facts pertaining to the first Waldorf school in Germany. This is important because Waldorf schools look not only to what Steiner said, but to what he did. Steiner was the director of the first Waldorf school, and he was hired by factory owner Emil Molt. He believed schools should be self-administered (a direct translation of his phrase; see Staley 1998), not administered by the state. Somehow, in finding its way to American soil, "self-administered" became "faculty-run," a clear semantic difference; and the consequences for the growth of Waldorf education are real. Through the 1970s and 1980s, schools (following a "third generation" countercultural model) distanced themselves almost pathologically from anything that smacked of authority, to the point where many then spoke of a "leadership crisis" in Waldorf schools. In the last twenty years or so, schools have hired non-teaching administrators to smooth day-to-day operations. Faculties generally retain significant control over an administrator, however; and, while operations may be easier, talk of a leadership or governance crisis continues.

Two Funnels

Cutting across the generations I have described in this history are two complementary, funnel-shaped changes. In the early days of Waldorf education, all teacher training was "on the job." People like the

Hales of Boston could go to Switzerland for three weeks, and then return to give anthroposophic lectures. You can imagine that there was a much greater variety of method, technique, application, and classroom experience both for teachers and for students. The first change I wish to describe, then, is one from this variety to a rough standardization of curriculum and method. Neither state is necessarily better than the other. Standardization implies quality control, respectability, and replicability; but it can also mean a loss of flexibility, and a door to dogma.

The second change is the change from a purely private, independent education to a variety of possibilities, including public charter and choice schools, organized home schooling groups and curricula, and at least one juvenile corrections institute that employs Waldorf methods. With few exceptions, students came from well-to-do white families in the early days—certainly no more than at other liberal, progressive but private schools. Although this is still largely the case, it is not entirely so. As with the first change, there are both possibilities and challenges associated with this added variety. Recovering a social mission and serving a larger variety of students are healthy possibilities for Waldorf education at present; although the dangers of dilution and misrepresentation become increasingly distinct.

The Futures of Waldorf Education

There are roughly fifty-three million K-12 school children in the United States. Of this number, forty-four million (83 percent) attend public schools. A few more than six million (11 percent) attend independent (private) schools. These numbers have remained fairly consistent over the past couple of decades.

Approximately 1.5 million (3 percent) are homeschooled, a number that has grown significantly in the past decade and that continues to grow. Homeschooling, however, seems generally to be a reaction against available options (public or private) rather than a positive choice in itself. Can it represent a viable future for educating children in the United States? I don't believe so. How much will this number grow? It's hard to say, but economic, political, and cultural pressures all suggest that it can't grow much more.

About 1.1 million (2 percent) attend charter schools; this number is growing, but given the grassroots energy required, and the opposition of school districts and teachers' unions, also seems unlikely to be a route to the solution of educational ills in the United States. Again, this number may grow significantly in years to come, but it is unlikely to increase by an order of magnitude.

Finally, lumping independent and public/charter Waldorf school students together yields a number around 25,000 to 30,000, or 1/18 of 1 percent (.06 percent) of students in the United States, and perhaps 1/2 of 1 percent of private school students. Betty Staley and others "on the ground" in California and on the West Coast of the United States, where Waldorf charter schools are most abundant and growing fastest, predict that within a few short years, there will be more students in public Waldorf charter schools than there are in independent Waldorf schools. This possibility has implications for the Association of Waldorf Schools of North America (AWSNA) and for the Alliance for Public Waldorf Education (APWE). It probably does not have implications for the overall configuration of education in the United States; a growth from 1/20 of 1 percent to 1/10 of 1 percent is not especially relevant.

The number of independent Waldorf schools, which grew at a rate approximately doubling every ten years from the 1930s through the 1990s, appears to be leveling off. The curve is becoming sigmoid, or "S" shaped; such a curve is sometimes called a saturation curve. That is, given the configurations of people's lives across roughly the past century, the demand for small, independent, relatively expensive, alternative Waldorf schools may be reaching its limit. Waldorf schools of this type may have saturated their possible markets. The number of Waldorf high schools has roughly tripled in the last decade, from a dozen to nearly forty, but this growth, too appears to be slowing.

It also seems like the failure rate for Waldorf schools may be increasing. It was low, a handful of schools, through the first six decades in the United States. I don't have numbers here; they're hard to come by. But it does seem like the conditions for the growth of new schools has changed. Maybe they're being founded in some new, less hardy way. Or maybe the cultural and economic climate has changed. Or maybe the way they represent Waldorf education has become unpalatable. Or perhaps AWSNA's trademark on the name Waldorf actually serves to depress the number of schools that are founded. Regardless, it's certainly true that service "industries" (like education) can't benefit from economies of scale; hence the increasing cost of all education.

This is not to say that new private Waldorf schools won't continue to be founded, but that their survival will be less assured, their road to sustainability harder. Without some fundamental change in how Waldorf schools see themselves and conduct themselves; or without some fundamental change in the conditions in which they exist, their growth henceforth will be arithmetic, let's say; not geometric, as it was in the twentieth century.

If the path to the future includes growth, it is likely not private school growth. Perhaps it's public school growth. There are between thirty and forty Waldorf charter schools in the United States. (Some call them "Waldorf inspired," but I don't care for this distinction.) The number is likely to continue to grow as the charter movement grows. But for how long will this be true? What is the saturation of charter schooling in the United States? Urban districts can absorb charter schools, but rural districts cannot. Charter schooling seems not to be a panacea for public education in the United States, and therefore not a permanent growth area for Waldorf schools.

Homeschooling, too, is burgeoning, and many homeschoolers receive an education that is based on Steiner's educational ideas. How many homeschoolers use Waldorf methods, and how they interpret them, is impossible to say.

Altogether, however, charter schools and homeschoolers represent fewer than three million school-age children. In 2010 there were roughly 35 California charter schools that used Waldorf methods and approximately 700 charters state-wide. So approximately ½ of one percent of charter school students in California are in Waldorf schools. This is an order of magnitude more than the roughly 1/20 of one percent of students nationwide who are in Waldorf schools. If the number of charters grows significantly, and if Waldorf methods grow as a constant percentage within this growth, then charter schools may represent the most significant possibility for the growth of the number of students receiving an education based on Steiner's ideas.

In the long run, however (the next decade or beyond), it seems unlikely that charter schools and homeschoolers offer real solutions to whatever ails U.S. education. These movements exist within the framework of intractable teachers' unions, increasing education costs, and pressure toward standardization from Washington that seems not to change from administration to administration. Here the crystal ball grows cloudy, not just for the future of Waldorf schooling, but for the future of schooling in the United States in general.

Patrice Maynard, Outreach Coordinator for AWSNA, and Gary Lamb, an independent scholar, are pursuing what we might call "the separation of school and state," based on their understanding of Steiner's call for culture to be administered separately from economic and political interests. Maynard is clear that if the virtual monopoly held by public schools were dissolved, there would be more room for greater experiment and diversity in efforts to educate children; and that more of these efforts would be likely to move in the directions that we presently call "Waldorf education." Assuming the unlikely success of such an effort in the short term—the next few decades, let's say—it is unclear how education would be funded absent property tax. Further, some Waldorf teacher educators see the crisis in public education as so dire that, given a small push, the rush to Waldorf education (indicated already by the growth of Waldorf charter schools in California) might become a stampede.

All of this may or may not be. What is more likely is an impending crisis for independent education in the United States in general; schools that are not supported by a tax base, and that cannot rely on economies of scale are becoming and will become increasingly expensive, relative to the costs of other things like food, shelter, and clothing. As long as we believe that a good education consists primarily of a couple of dozen students and a teacher in a purpose-built building, small independent schools without endowments will be challenged first. And most Waldorf schools fit this category. Larger independent schools will be challenged soon after. But this challenge isn't exclusive to independent schools; as taxpayers are asked to pay more and more to support public schools, public schools, too, will be forced to change.

The solutions here are not clear, although they must exist; children will need to be educated no matter how dire the future of educational funding. Some may leap instantly to thoughts of technology, distance learning, online learning, and so on, but it's clear that those who value education may see human relationships as central to the endeavor; they don't necessarily support technological fixes, or the dehumanizing removal of a teacher from a student's presence.

I think, sometimes, of a former student of mine, a well-educated woman from India. During a discussion of U.S. class size, more than thirty students in a public school classroom was lamented as being "just too many"; half that was preferable. The student from India volunteered, "In my elementary school years, I was never in a class of fewer than sixty-five students." There may be more creative ways to work toward keeping educational costs down than increasing class size: sharing community resources and buildings among schools and other groups, for example. But the challenge is one that faces us all, whether independent school or public school.

Current and foreseeable challenges to education, including specifically to Waldorf education, do not actually provide any real basis for prognostication. On the one hand, it is possible in the not-too-distant future that all independent Waldorf schools, accompanied by other small, unendowed private schools, will simply go out of business. Other challenges could as soon do away with public Waldorf schools. On the other hand, several teacher educators mentioned to me that it is possible, given the violence, meaninglessness, political interference, and even dehumanization of much in public education today, Waldorf schools of all sorts—public and private—will thrive in that they offer an alternative or antidote to some of these ailments. The dangers of extrapolation are well known, and the actual course of Waldorf schools in the United States will undoubtedly fall somewhere between collapse and triumph; this hardly constitutes a prediction.

To the degree that parents want the best for their children, and that Rudolf Steiner's ideas about education (about how children learn and how teachers may teach them; about the humanizing influence of education; and about the place and role of humanity in the world) are true and valuable, it seems likely that Waldorf schools of one kind or another will continue not merely to exist but to grow. Teachers' and parents' ingenuity, good will, and diligence will ensure that students can receive an education based on these ideas and these methods, by whatever name, for the foreseeable future.

PART II

WALDORF EDUCATION as METHOD and MYTH

Note: The following three chapters are formed from four articles that appeared in the Waldorf Education *Research Bulletin* between 2002 and 2009. The first chapter, in modified form, also appeared as a portion of the introduction to the book, *What is Waldorf Education?* (2003).

7. RECOVERING THE QUALITY OF WALDORF EDUCATION

"WALDORF EDUCATION" DOES NOT EXIST. It is not a "thing" and it is not a brand (although various groups own trademarks on its name in different countries). Rudolf Steiner did not intend to create a small coterie of private schools, or even a large group of public schools. When he spoke about teaching and learning, he spoke about teaching and learning; not about Waldorf teachers teaching, or Waldorf students learning. More about this below.

Because Waldorf education does not exist, it cannot be found in the boxes we call Waldorf schools. To narrow its definition to identify it with schools named Waldorf or Steiner schools, or to identify it with a particular curriculum or technique, is to reify Waldorf education in a way that may describe part of what is, but necessarily ignores what may also be. What we call Waldorf education may perhaps be found in any school, or anywhere that teachers teach and students learn. There is no characteristic or quality that is unique to what we call Waldorf education that cannot potentially be found somewhere else. Waldorf education, as an idea or set of ideas, slips through the cracks of any structure erected to define it.

In writing that "there is no such thing as Waldorf education," I am alluding to psychiatrist Donald Winnicott's famous statement that there is "no such thing as a baby" (1996), which has been followed through decades by other healthy attempts to overcome the fragmenting, objectifying tendencies of our modern minds. Winnicott was at pains to show, in England after World War II, that a child alone cannot survive without a mother, at least (or, to use more contemporary language, without a caregiver). His research into the necessary, life-giving, and life-sustaining relationship of child and parent added significantly to what we know about children and childhood. Clearly, he was not actually denying the existence of children in any but a rhetorical sense. In fact, he devoted much of his life and career to them. Similarly, my claim that there is no such thing as Waldorf education is meant as a rhetorical device, but one that I intend to use seriously.

To view Waldorf education as a thing-in-itself is necessarily to see it partially and inaccurately. To believe in things as entities separate from context and the rest of creation is to participate in exactly the fragmenting, objectifying consciousness against which Waldorf teachers wish to stand. Further, as we have seen, to identify Waldorf education by its trappings, practices, or functions is to see it only superficially.

Just as Waldorf education has no definite boundaries, it also has no definite origin. We may describe Waldorf education, for example, as arising from the educational conceptions of Rudolf Steiner. But many of his concepts—for example, the idea that, culturally, at least, "ontogeny recapitulates phylogeny" (the development of an individual mirrors in microcosm the development of the species)—may be shown to be older than Steiner and therefore not to have originated with him. Beyond inferences from Steiner's work, it is difficult to discover the idea that "the" Waldorf curriculum must include Norse myths in fourth grade or Greek history in fifth grade (these are curricular practices common in Waldorf schools). The idea is not in well-known lecture cycles that he gave on education, nor is it in *Foundations of Human Experience* (also published under the title *Study of Man*) and its correlates; nor may it be found in Stockmeyer's or Heydebrand's well-known descriptions of German Waldorf school curricula. It's not that these ideas are correct or incorrect; it's that they are not unique to Steiner's work.

In writing the preceding paragraphs, I don't mean at all to minimize Steiner's contributions to thinking about education. I mean two things: I mean to see his work in a larger context, and I mean to point to an aspect of his genius worth noting: his astonishing ability to synthesize vast and disparate portions of human knowing and understanding.

Emerson and the Waldorf Curriculum

For the United States, the writings of Ralph Waldo Emerson, who lived a generation before Steiner, contain in prototypical form many of Steiner's ideas about education. Emerson's essay "History," for example, presents an encapsulated curriculum that mirrors closely the general curriculum of many Waldorf schools. His language, too, mirrors Steiner's in addressing the intellectual and emotional maturation of one person as a partial recapitulation of the intellectual and cultural developments to be found in human history.

The following quotations from "History" demonstrate the correspondence that Emerson finds between history and individual growth and development. This evolution of ideas is presumably based on knowledge of ancient cultures, or at least exposure to them. Someone who had never heard of the Greeks, nor been exposed to their cultural influence even in a dilute or adulterated form, could not be expected in ontogeny to recapitulate this aspect of a cultural phylogeny. On the other hand, as Emerson implies at the end of the first two quotations, the state of being Greek, in the sense of "the spiritual nature unfolded in strict unity with the body," may be universally human, even for those who do not name it by the same name Emerson uses:

What is the foundation of that interest all men feel in Greek history, letters, art and poetry, in all its periods from the Homeric age down to the domestic life of the Athenians and Spartans, four or five centuries later? What but this, that every man passes personally through a Grecian period. The Grecian state is the era of the bodily nature, the perfection of the senses—of the spiritual nature unfolded in strict unity with the body. (123)

In many Waldorf school fifth grades, when teachers claim students have achieved a grace and harmony of body and spirit that will soon be disrupted by the travails of puberty and adolescence, the class holds a Greek "Olympiad," competing for laurels in javelin, discus and running races, striving as much for form and beauty as for victory. Greek myths, as well, make up a significant portion of the literature of the fifth grade in many Waldorf schools.

The comparison between Emerson's writings and Steiner's is a study in itself. One more example will suffice here. For both Steiner and Emerson, the study of nature can guide and give meaning to personal experience. Neither means by nature what we might call "environmental studies," although these would not be excluded; each means that symbolic meaning may be found in the reflective examination of the world around us.

It is essential that the secrets of Nature, the laws of life be taught to the boy or girl, not in dry intellectual concepts, but as far as possible in symbols. Parables of the spiritual connections of things should be brought before the soul of the child in such a manner that behind the parable the child divines and feels, rather than grasps intellectually, the underlying law of all existence. "All that is passing is but a parable," must be the maxim guiding all our education in this [elementary school] period. (Steiner 1965, 33)

Here is Emerson on the same topic:

I can symbolize my thought by using the name of any creature, of any fact, because every creature is man, agent or patient. Tantalus means the impossibility of drinking the waters of thought which are always gleaming and waving within sight of the soul. ...Every animal of the barn-yard, the field and the forest, of the earth and the waters that are under the earth, has contrived to get a footing and to leave the print of its features and form in some one or other of these upright, heaven-facing speakers. (2000, 127)

Steiner's thinking is often prefigured in Emerson's, but this is not to say that they are the same. Toward the end of his essay "Education," Emerson (1966) tosses in a towel that Steiner held onto like a bulldog: "I confess myself utterly at a loss in suggesting particular reforms in our ways of teaching" (225). Steiner, in concert with Emil Molt and a host of others, set out to reform our ways of teaching in a myriad of concrete ways. But, while broad and systematic, few or none of these ways were as original as we might believe, nor were they meant to be particular to some schools and not others.

A Unique Method?

Separate from the ideas in or behind Steiner's concept of education, we might describe Waldorf education as a particular method. When we define method, however, we omit important elements of Steiner's thinking. And certainly in the case of Waldorf education, we are not talking about a collection of techniques or a bag of tricks, but a method in a larger sense. As Michael Lipson, recent translator of Steiner's *Intuitive Thinking as a Spiritual Path*, put it, somewhat cryptically, Steiner's method is a "methodless method" that must be continually re-invented by each teacher for each student in order to be valid (2002). And if we use a more mundane definition of method, and speak of a particular curriculum or set of teaching techniques, Waldorf education still eludes capture. Schools that are not Waldorf schools and teachers who are not Waldorf teachers use (and perhaps increasingly so) techniques and concepts of education identical to those propounded by Steiner, even though many of these teachers may never have heard Steiner's name. "Looping," in which one teacher stays with a particular class for several years; and block scheduling, in which one subject is studied intensively for a relatively brief time, are two such techniques. While no other school of which I know even approximates the curriculum found in a typical Waldorf school, there is nothing to prevent such adoption.

The Doctor Didn't Say

One step toward recognizing that there is no such thing as Waldorf education is to realize that Rudolf Steiner himself rarely spoke or wrote about Waldorf education. The annotated bibliography of his collected works lists only a small handful of references to *Waldorfschulpaedagogik*, "Waldorf School pedagogy," meaning not "Waldorf education" in the sense we generally take it today, but with specific reference to the way education was practiced at the (then) only Waldorf school, the Independent Waldorf School in Stuttgart, Germany.

Steiner did speak and write at great length about education: how children grow and develop and learn, and how teachers may teach them. Further, in his work, Steiner claimed no particular originality. He did not see a discontinuity between what came before him and his own work. In *The Education of the Child* (1996a), for example, Steiner quotes Jean Paul approvingly and at length. The sense one gets reading Steiner's work is that ideas, like apples, lead an objective existence, and may be plucked by anyone. This sense applies to his writings and lectures on matters other than education, as well. We might say that the "method" of Waldorf education is to learn to pluck these apples for oneself, as student or teacher, and not to rely on the authority of Rudolf Steiner to hand one already-picked apples. The analogy holds in that we may no more reify Waldorf education than we may divorce apples from the tree, sun, soil of their birth. Ideas, like apples, exist in and arise out of a context.

Compromise

Don't take my word for Steiner's wishes, by the way. Here are two quotations that make his positions clear:

> Moreover, I should like to point out to you that the real aim and object of our education is not to found as many schools as possible... but our education concerns itself with methods of teaching, and it is essentially a new way and art of education, so every teacher can bring it into their work in whatever kind of school they happen to be... and I have declared that the methods can be introduced into every situation where someone has the good will to do it. (Steiner, R. *The Roots of Education*, 30)

> Another aspect is that the crux of Anthroposophical education is its method. The schools apply a certain method. It is not a question of any particular political direction but purely and simply of method. It is also not a question of any particular religious creed, or of seeing anthroposophy somehow as a religious creed. It is simply a question of method.
>
> In the discussion that followed my lecture cycles, my answer to questions on this was simply that the educational method represented here can be applied anywhere, wherever there is the good will to introduce it.

If this is done on the one hand, and if on the other hand in order to create an understanding in wider circles—it is clearly emphasized that this is the proper method and that it is being applied in a school that can serve as a model, if these two points are given the main emphasis in the program, if it is stressed that every school could use these methods and that a model school could demonstrate how fruitful they are, and if things are worked out neatly, then I believe that something could be achieved even in Switzerland. [Steiner was speaking in Switzerland as he said this.] And then on the basis of these two points educational associations ought to be founded everywhere. But it would have to be made clear to everyone that the aim was not to found as many private schools as possible to compete with the state schools. In Switzerland such a thing would be regarded as something very peculiar and it would never be understood. But there would be an understanding for a model school which could be a source of inspiration for a method of education. Progress cannot be made in any other way. It is important to present these things to people in principle again and again and wherever the opportunity arises.

I believe it would be a good thing if you could always give the greatest prominence to these two aspects. They are perfectly true, and much damage has been done to us by the constant repetition of the view that Waldorf education can only be carried out in schools apart from the main stream, whereas I have constantly repeated that the methods can be applied in any school.

This is what I wanted to say, for everything else is linked to this. I also believe that a financial basis will only be won when there can be an understanding of these things. There will be very little under-standing in Switzerland for independent schools if they are not linked to what I have just been saying. But if this is done, I believe that our efforts could lead to greater success than has been the case hitherto. (Excerpt from *The Christmas Conference for the Foundation of the General Anthroposophical Society 1923/24* (1990, 167-169.)

Some will acknowledge the validity of these passages, but insist on a distinction between those who employ a "compromised" version of Steiner's method ("Waldorf-inspired" or "Waldorf methods" schools or teachers) and "real" Waldorf schools that have deliberately dedicated themselves to this method. I maintain, however, that all manifestations of Rudolf Steiner's educational ideas are necessarily compromised. Schools that see themselves as pure because they are independent of the potentially corrupting influence of government money may be compared with schools (like the Milwaukee Urban Waldorf School, a choice school within the Milwaukee public school system) that have made overt compromises to meet present requirements regarding the separation of church and state. (One of these compromises has been to eliminate the word "God" from a verse that children in the school say each morning.) The Milwaukee school's compromise is a deliberate choice made in order to facilitate other educational objectives, especially the education of relatively poor urban children. Independent (non-public) Waldorf schools, on the other hand, have clearly chosen, if not so deliberately, not to serve poor and near-poor students like those who attend the Milwaukee school. This choice is also a compromise.

THREE OF A KIND: STRATEGIES AND DESCRIPTIONS

A First Strategy: Waldorf Schools ARE Waldorf Education

Existing descriptions of Waldorf education can be characterized according to three strategies. The first and simplest is to let Waldorf schools stand for a description; what goes on in Waldorf schools is inferred to be, by definition, Waldorf education. Ida Oberman's otherwise excellent history, *Fidelity and Flexibility in Waldorf Education, 1919-1998*, slips into this mode, examining the histories of Waldorf schools in Germany and the United States, implying that these add up to a larger history of Waldorf education. To further her discussion she uses the concept of a "cultural field," a metaphorical container for Waldorf education. Just as the field is a metaphor, so too is Waldorf education.

Stephen Talbott also uses this first strategy in an appendix to the also otherwise excellent book *The Future Does Not Compute*. He asks, "What is Waldorf Education?" and answers with a description of the founding of the first school and a description of a generalized curriculum (424).

If Waldorf education were a consistent and prescribed method and curriculum, these analogies might suffice, although their definition is circular. But what goes on in Waldorf schools varies from place to place and time to time. There is no single characteristic, in fact, without which a Waldorf school cannot exist, nor that defines a school as a Waldorf school. Mentally erase beeswax crayons, or a eurythmist, or even the morning verse. A school without these items could still fulfill Steiner's wishes for the education of children, I believe. Waldorf education simply cannot be seen as the accumulation or collection of some (even infinite) number of defining characteristics. To indulge such a fragmented view is to give credence to a reductionism that Waldorf education stands against.

A Second Strategy: Pigeonholes

The second strategy is to pigeonhole Waldorf education according to some cultural or historical characteristic that, while real enough within a particular context, may not be necessary or sufficient to describe something larger called Waldorf education. Waldorf education is defined only partially if it is defined as a reform movement, for example. To the extent that authors acknowledge the contingency of such synecdochical definitions (definitions in which the part stands for the whole), they may be serviceable, if incomplete.

Henry Barnes and the Movement

Henry Barnes, author and long-time history teacher and faculty chairman at the Rudolf Steiner School in New York City, characterizes Waldorf education as a particular movement: "As one of the most rapidly growing yet least known independent, nonsectarian school movements in the free world today, Rudolf Steiner or Waldorf education should be brought to the attention of all serious students of education" (1980, 323). This may be true, but Waldorf education is "independent" [of public education in the United States] and a "movement" only in the here and now.

Barnes writes, "This article will briefly outline the history of the Waldorf movement and seek to give an introduction to the philosophy and methods that underlie it" (323). Philosophy and methods sound promising; they may extend beyond consideration of Waldorf education as a movement. For Barnes, the philosophy is based on two major principles or insights. The primary or defining principle of Waldorf education is an image of the human being:

> Behind the Waldorf curriculum, its methods of instruction, and all the many practical aspects one thinks of when one thinks of a Waldorf school today stands the idea of man and of child development from which they all spring. It is this idea that gives them meaning and, in the end, is the basis on which the [Waldorf education] movement will have to be evaluated and judged. (326)

To speak of the education of a child necessarily implies a concept of what or who this child is. Historical examples abound, including Locke's "tabula rasa"; Rousseau's good "natural man" Emile; Jonathan Edwards' very different "natural man" in original sin; and Dewey's concept of the child in community. For Barnes, Waldorf schools attempt to educate according to Rudolf Steiner's image of a human being:

> In Steiner's view, the human being can never be fully understood in terms of his heredity and the impact of his environment. Beyond them lies the essential core of human individuality, which cannot be defined in material terms. That central entity, the human ego, is perceived by Steiner to be supersensible and eternal, revealing itself by reflection in the personality who is active here in time and space. It is the educator's responsibility to help this personality to develop in such a way that it can become a fitting vehicle through which the real ego can express itself. (326)

Note that Barnes refers to "educators" in the last sentence quoted, not to "Waldorf educators." The virtual brand name "Waldorf" is a label attached after Steiner, not by Steiner. The label "Waldorf" represents an increasing objectification of ideas that were initially less defined and therefore more open to play and experiment than they often seem.

The words "in Steiner's view" and "perceived by Steiner" are almost extraneous here. Steiner is certainly not the only nor the first person to speak of a human being as more than the sum of genes and environment. If he, and others who find the world this way, are correct, then inferences regarding education follow not from authority but from a perceived reality. Where reference to Steiner should be inserted in the quotation above is in the last sentence. "[For Steiner,] it is the educator's responsibility..." Even here, Steiner is not unique, although his lectures and writings certainly constitute the most thorough and systematic approach to education from this perspective.

Barnes's point is that according to Steiner, the "supersensible and eternal" incarnate in the world, gradually and in a specific fashion. Education, therefore, should be conducted in accordance with what is known about this process of incarnation. Hence, the methods and curricula derive from this view.

For Barnes's, a second principle grows from the first; because the human self is seen to incarnate over a period of years, education must address this development, which is seen to occur in three broad stages lasting roughly seven years each. (Many writers on Waldorf education treat these as if they were universal, when Steiner himself made it clear time and again that he was describing something that was historically and culturally true, rather than true everywhere and for all time.) The method and curriculum similarly derive from these principles, and provide the particulars visible to any visitor to a Waldorf school, including instructional materials and subject matter. These will likely include relatively featureless rag dolls, beeswax crayons, watercolor paints, colored chalk, stories of Christian saints, Norse and Greek Myths, and any number of other things. But the rhetorical question still remains: does any of these make a Waldorf school? Barnes's consideration of methods and philosophy extends his definition beyond the merely synecdochical, but his discussion here speaks best to education in general, not to "Waldorf" education.

Oberman's Objectification

Ida Oberman's history of Waldorf education also offers an objectified view. For her, "Waldorf" is a "unique" "German" "progressive" "alternative" "reform initiative" or "institution" which has "embedded" in it "an ideology, a belief system called Anthroposophy." All of these descriptions may apply to "Waldorf education," but each could change radically without disturbing Steiner's contributions to ways of teaching.

Oberman locates sources for the curriculum of the first Waldorf school in Steiner's intellectual biography; but having shown the curriculum's somewhat contingent nature, then treats it as an object to be relocated wherever "Waldorf" roots. Oberman shows how different people (Hermann von Baravalle, Marie Steiner, and Ita Wegman) and different schools (the Rudolf Steiner School in New York City, the Kimberton Waldorf School, and the Sacramento Waldorf School) adopt different strategies ("purity," "accommodation," and "evolution"); but not how curricula reflect their origins in Steiner's work and in the time and place of their implementation.

Among the evidence for this point of view is Oberman's insertion of the bracketed qualifier "Waldorf" into a quotation in which it did not originally appear: "The faculty now active at the school have proven... their willingness to continue this [Waldorf] work, which represents the noblest of German cultural life for all to see" (Emil Molt and Duke Fritz von Bothmer quoted in Oberman 1999, 134). It is clear that Oberman, who inserted the word "Waldorf" in brackets in the quotation above, sees the work as Waldorf work, but this is her own objectification. We should be careful, I believe, not to follow her and others in this direction.

More amusingly, in at least one place, Oberman refers to those who practice, or believe in, or aim to further Waldorf education as "Waldorfers." My students call them "Waldorfians" or "Steinerites." Students at one Waldorf high school produced pale blue t-shirts emblazoned in white, "Waldork." Less amusingly, children of Waldorf teachers, left on their own while the teachers meet and meet, are sometimes referred to as "Waldorphans."

A Third Strategy: School Functions

A third strategy involves some function or group of functions that Waldorf education performs (is claimed to perform). If the difficulty of the last definition is that it is too narrow ("what is" does not define "what else may be") the difficulty of a functional definition is that it is too broad. Good education of any kind will necessarily perform certain functions that cannot simply be claimed only for, let's say, Waldorf education. Waldorf teachers are not the only teachers to claim a developmental view of their students; nor are they the only ones to find some aspects of human individuality that cannot be attributed solely to the interaction of heredity and the environment. Further, it does not appear that there is some unique set of functions that only something called Waldorf education performs.

Eugene Schwartz's Functionalism

For Eugene Schwartz, Waldorf education is a method, based on the work of Rudolf Steiner, who "begins with a qualitative intelligence that is unitary and suggests that the task of education is to multiply it. If [Howard] Gardner's theory concerns itself with 'multiple intelligences,' then Steiner's approach might be called 'intelligent multiplicity'" (151). Further, Schwartz describes Waldorf education as a "'will first' pedagogy" or "methodology" that aims to "educate the child in accordance with principles that ask us to honor and work with the soul and spiritual nature of the youngster" (157). While this sounds vague, it is only his introduction into a more specific examination of methods and techniques that teachers may use.

As for setting these ideas in a context as large as that of Barnes or Curran (see below), I don't believe Schwartz sees this as a helpful goal; his more immediately practical goal is to show how Waldorf education can function to address the needs of children in a particular place and time. That is, he is concerned with the "will" education of children in wealthy industrialized countries.

A Look at the Map

Eugene Schwartz also approaches the function of Waldorf education by analogy. Like a map, Schwartz posits, a curriculum can be understood on three levels. The first, a global, geophysical map, remains valid for centuries. For Schwartz, Steiner's description of child development is such a durable aspect of Waldorf education. Development itself may change, but only slowly. School subjects such as history, math, and so forth, change more rapidly, and have been modified significantly over the decades since Waldorf education began. These are akin to a political map, which may change more rapidly. An up-to-date road map, however, must "come alive every day." The clear advantage of Schwartz's analogy is that it neatly allows both for relatively unchanging aspects, and for the continually changing aspects of Waldorf education. One danger of this view, however, is that agreement on the unchanging aspects of the map may be perceived as dogma: unchanging and therefore unquestioned. The history of geology shows, however, that while the earth appears to change slowly, our views and interpretations of that change can be revised radically from one year to the next. The notion that Waldorf education is a thing, however immaterial, has developed so surreptitiously over the past decades that we have not noticed the change. Our map has not changed much, perhaps, but we may be in danger of mistaking the map for the thing itself.

A Quality of Education

Each of the strategies outlined above makes Waldorf education into a thing, whether a material thing like a school, or an ideological thing like a movement, or a mental thing like a function. Not all writers on Waldorf education, however, resort to these three strategies. Those who perceive Waldorf education not as a thing but as a quality of education demonstrate a different possibility for description.

Peter Curran on Waldorf Education

Peter Curran, graduate of Bowdoin College and longtime history teacher at The Waldorf School of Garden City, adopts a strategy similar to Barnes's in describing Waldorf education, but then ventilates it immediately to include, potentially, all schools, not a particular subset. Following his retirement in the late 1980s, Curran set down some of his ideas about Waldorf schools. Particularly, he believed that there were four "essentials," "without which no school (by whatever name) is a Waldorf School and with which any school is a Waldorf School."

I.   …As each child's consciousness matures, it recapitulates the cultural epochs of all Mankind. Waldorf education agrees with Emerson when he says that all children go through a Greek period and a Roman period, etc. There is, then, a proper time and method for particular subjects to be taught.

II. Since no one destroys what one loves, reverence, awe and respect for the Earth should be fostered. An inkling of the spirituality of the Earth then comes into being.

III. The qualitative, as well as the quantitative, in all things should be equally developed.

IV. Above all, Man is known as a spiritual as well as a physical being.

Curran's statement poses a realism to Barnes's nominalism in that the enactment of these principles does not depend on the presence or absence of the name "Waldorf."

Of Curran's four principles, the first and last are potentially controversial, while the middle two may be found in many classrooms and schools. The first, the "ontogeny recapitulates phylogeny" statement, is probably the least familiar to most educators, and it may be the most dated, arising out of Aristotle's "Great Chain of Being." (See, for example, Lovejoy, 1936 and 1964.) Few, if any schools other than Waldorf schools, now organize themselves around such a principle. Still, there is nothing to prevent them doing so if they choose. (Nor, if Waldorf schools found a different central metaphor, would they necessarily cease to be good schools.)

Last, some contemporary interpretations of the anti-establishment of religion clause of the First Amendment to the U.S. Constitution might prevent Curran's fourth principle from being overtly applied in public schools, but the concept is hardly unique among independent schools. Some Waldorf teachers may argue that principle four may be found in many schools, but that Waldorf schools mean something different by "spirit." I'm not convinced of this, however; and in any event, it needn't be so.

Douglas Sloan's "Education of the Imagination"

Douglas Sloan, retired Professor of History and Education at Teachers College, New York, worked diligently through writing and teaching to present an open-minded approach to Waldorf education. In *Insight-Imagination*, he describes Waldorf education sensitively in his discussion of a larger "education of the imagination" (1983, 211).

Maurice Merleau-Ponty (1964) wrote of the "primacy of perception": "all consciousness is perceptual, even the consciousness of ourselves... The perceived world is the always presupposed foundation of
all rationality, all value and all existence" (13). For Sloan, the faculty of
"imagination" necessarily accompanies perception, without which we
would live in William James' "buzzing, blooming confusion." For Sloan,
imagination is not simply one faculty among others (empathy or cognition, say) to be strengthened through an enhanced curriculum. Imagination is the necessary wellspring of human experience of the world:

> ...it is only through imagination that we have any knowledge what-
> soever....The imagination, the image-making power of the mind ...
> shapes our everyday perception of the world, for there is no percep-
> tion separate from interpretation. (140)

Similarly to Barnes, Sloan describes Waldorf education according to a
concept of educational stages. After briefly examining Piaget with regard
to stages, however, Sloan qualifies his statements: "Any conception of educational stages must... stand constantly ready to be reevaluated and revised
in the light of new evidence from any field of research..." (212). For Sloan,
Waldorf education does not approach a faith, nor was it created ready-
made by Rudolf Steiner, to be preserved in perpetuity like a Colonial
reenactment. "Such a conception of education must as a whole remain
open and subject to revision..." (212). Waldorf education is an evolving
model of educational thinking, research, and practice, and must be created
anew in each application if it is not to devolve into prescription or dogma.

Nancy Parsons Whittaker's Open Door Policy

Nancy Parsons Whittaker is a translator of Steiner's work into English,
and a founder and administrator of "www.bobnancy.com," a website
devoted to Waldorf education. The paragraphs that follow do not set
forth a thing-like definition, but attempt to throw open the doors of a
somewhat cloistered "movement":

> I believe that the educational movement Steiner founded drifted
> very far from its source the moment [the act of] founding schools

became more important than examining the quality of education the children were receiving and working to really convey the approach to other teachers in all manner of schools and situations. What we call "Waldorf Education" has largely come to mean a set of curricula and specific ways of introducing specific subject matter. This has nothing (in my opinion) to do with the original intent, which was to convey the attitude, the viewpoint toward the children and toward society (any society) with which a teacher could fully meet the physical, mental and spiritual needs of both the students and their community.

Any school is a Waldorf school if the intent of Steiner's pedagogy is being met within its halls. What was the intent? The intent was to offer an education in a way that gave each child a fundamental, true introduction into the foundation of his or her society while at the same time enhancing that child's ability to accurately perceive life around him or her without damaging the child's innate capacity to be sensitively aware of the Creative Love behind the visible world (whatever that capacity might have been, whether large, small or nearly nonexistent—the teaching was not intended to train a student's spiritual vision, just not to damage what already existed). The education was not intended to found schools separated from their society at large nor was it intended to model a particular belief system.

These goals can be met in a wide variety of settings, with an infinitely wide possibility of curricula, through the myriad possibilities of human personality. (2001)

A Lack of Definition

Those who aim deliberately not to objectify Waldorf education can avoid the pitfalls of reification, synecdoche, or function. These writers necessarily leave Waldorf education undefined, and characterize it in refreshingly open terms. Waldorf education becomes not a thing, not a kind or brand of education, but a quality of education. And qualities, like colors, like the warmth of a heart, may expand boundlessly.

Speaking of warmth of heart, Steiner relates the following anecdote about his time in the Waldorf School: "Whenever I come to Stuttgart to visit and assist in the guidance of the school, I ask the same question in each class, naturally within the appropriate context and avoiding any possible tedium, 'Children, do you love your teachers?' You should hear and witness the enthusiasm with which they call out in chorus, 'Yes!' This call to the teachers to engender love within their pupils is all part of the question of how the older generation should relate to the young" (2003, 133).

Can we imagine a school today—even a Waldorf school—in which it is safe to ask that question? Can we imagine a person, teacher or not, who could safely ask such a question? Would the children's answers be the same?

8. PLAYING "STEINER SAYS": TWENTY-TWO MYTHS ABOUT WALDORF EDUCATION

READERS WHO KNOW SOMETHING of what goes on in Waldorf schools may read the foregoing, but object, "What about...?" Ron Grele (Chair of the Oral History Project at Columbia University) said, when I mentioned my book to him, "Steiner—isn't there some sort of diet that goes with that?" He was referring to the fact that Steiner favored vegetarianism in an age when that was more of a fad than it is currently. I don't address vegetarianism below (it doesn't bear directly on education) but I do address some of the more common misperceptions about what we call Waldorf education.

To begin, two stories.

During my first year or two of teaching, our faculty meeting enjoyed the presence of two eminent European Waldorf teachers. My recollection is that one came from the United Kingdom and one from Germany, but that doesn't matter. One appeared in the fall and one in the spring. The first, answering a colleague's question, said, "You should never use tongue-twisters; they trivialize language." Heads nodded. The second, also in response to a colleague's question, replied, "Of course, the best possible thing for that is to recite tongue twisters with your class." Heads nodded again. And there we were, back where we belonged, on our own recognizance. Two experts, two apparently contradictory points of view. Presumably, both were based on considered interpretations of Steiner's work.

Steiner, by the way, advocated speech exercises that are, in fact, tongue twisters. I don't know the context in which one expert opposed their use. Perhaps he or she had observed this particular teacher in action, or believed the rhymes in use were not doing the job Steiner intended. In any case, context is necessary to understand a recommendation without implementing it as a prescription, from which it is a small step to orthodoxy.

Years later, just when I thought I would be moving on to university teaching, I found myself happily teaching a seventh grade. An otherwise bright girl, who later graduated high in her prep school class, could not multiply or divide fractions. I asked her why not. Her reply: "Because whenever I try, I just see gnomes dancing and spinning on the page." What? Somehow I had managed to teach in Waldorf schools for nearly twenty years without encountering "math gnomes" and their relatives, including "King Plus" and "Queen Minus." I had read Rudolf Steiner and Hermann von Baravalle on teaching math, and had no recollection of these gnomes or anything like them. It occurred to me that a lot of what we do in Waldorf schools each day (and sometimes have to explain or defend to colleagues or parents) has little or no basis in Steiner's work. I've since said, seriously, that gnomes have better work to do than to teach little boys and girls about arithmetic operations.

Understandably, but not necessarily happily, Waldorf education is known primarily by its external characteristics or trappings, characteristics about which, surprisingly often, Steiner himself had little or nothing to say. Or what he had to say about teaching and learning is not what we find in practice today. Or what he had to say leaves open many more possibilities than are available in practice today.

Researching what someone—Steiner—did *not* say is difficult. All one can do is read everything available, using a process of elimination to discover, for example, that Steiner's work contains no references to math gnomes or their ilk. The possibility remains that someone, somewhere, will discover a previously unknown reference that substantiates a previously unsubstantiated claim. At that point, the task becomes to assess the validity of the reference—was it written by Steiner? Recorded and transcribed? Revised by Steiner or not? Recorded verbatim or as a note? A diary entry? Part of an oral tradition? In what context does this reference sit? Was it given as a specific indication and then generalized beyond its original intent? Is it helpful or harmful that this has happened? On what merit may we adopt or shun this claim about teaching and learning?

Hermit crabs have no shells of their own, so they crawl into shells abandoned by other critters. Similarly, U.S. Waldorf schools, unable or unwilling to find a comfortable home in the plural cultures of the nation, have a tendency to crawl into the shell of a German or central European culture—or a partly remembered, partly imagined notion of that culture. Alternately, U.S. Waldorf schools sometimes crawl into an English shell, following the lead and model of Michael Hall and other established English Waldorf schools; or taking their lead from Anglophone translations of Steiner's work. I call this process of embellishing a foundational orthodoxy the "Hermit Crab Theory of Institutional History," because it applies also to institutions other than Waldorf schools, although I am not concerned with other institutions here.

An alternative to hermit crabbing, more challenging, is for Waldorf schools, as they grow and mature, to forge their own cultures more consciously. Each school would better serve its community. Schools would seem less superficially similar but could, in focusing on the essential, remain similar in ways that matter.

What follow are twenty myths about Waldorf education, beliefs, and practices that we find in many, if not most, Waldorf schools in the United States. I have an even longer list—this is the sort of list that can never really end—but focus here on the most prevalent or most interesting items, or those that may be presented in a brief essay.

Such a critique of Waldorf school practices immediately begs for a central question: If Waldorf education is not to be known by its trappings and myths, where is its core? What is essential to teaching and learning in Waldorf schools? I will address this question in the next chapter. Suffice it to say here that an excellent approach to such a question may also be found in Susan Howard's "The Essentials of Waldorf Early Childhood Education" (2006). It concerns early childhood teachers, but much of the content applies to teachers of all grades. Howard's method, too, may be fruitful for all teachers.

1. Alternative Education

Steiner's view was both narrower and broader than the collection of small independent schools and an even smaller group of charter schools that exist in the United States today. In total, they probably serve no more than 25,000 students. (New York City public schools alone serve one million.) Steiner wanted to promote the development, on the one hand, of model schools that would demonstrate to the world the validity of his method. On the other hand, he wanted to make this method available to whoever wished to implement it (1997). In the 1930s and 1940s, Waldorf schools in the United States arose more according to this scheme; while now Waldorf schools are seen largely as an alternative to mainstream or conventional education. The Rudolf Steiner School in New York City was, with the Dalton School and others, an active member of the Progressive Education Association (PEA) in the 1930s. These schools banded together, for example, to restrict the showing of violent newsreels prior to the start of movies in Upper East Side movie houses. The school also held a number of workshops and lectures, both in conjunction with the PEA and alone, to introduce Steiner's educational ideas to a broader audience. The Waldorf School of Garden City was founded as a "demonstration school" on the campus of Adelphi University. Further, as late as the 1970s, the Waldorf School of Garden City was a member of the Washington, D.C., based Council for Educational Freedom (CEF), a group that advocated, among other planks, work toward the separation of school and state.

The PEA no longer exists. The CEF still does, but the Waldorf School of Garden City is no longer a member. Nor is the Waldorf School of Garden City a "demonstration" school any longer. Since the 1960s and the 1970s, Waldorf schools have increasingly turned their foci inward, engaging with each other rather than with the larger world of education in the United States. In the absence of an association like the Association of Waldorf Schools of North America (AWSNA), and being low in numbers, it was more necessary for Waldorf schools in the early days to engage with other, non-anthroposophic educational institutions. Such engagement clarifies and strengthens mission and practice.

2. Artistic Teaching vs. Teaching Art

Too often, Steiner's call for artistic teaching is misunderstood as a call for art teaching. Any subject may be taught and learned in a creative way. A teacher with a particular gift in an art may impart more to her students by offering a broad and deep experience of that art than she would by trying to be all things to all students. Little bits of too much produce dilettantes. Artistic teaching is required especially to teach math, science, and subjects that might otherwise easily lose their vitality.

By artistic teaching I mean teaching that approaches the creative core of any particular subject, and that is truly educational and not merely instructive. A full treatment of what I mean by artistic teaching would include a full consideration of what Steiner describes in his work on teaching and learning, what is commonly called Waldorf education.

None of this is to say that teachers should not teach the arts; but that in the rush to include everything, it is possible for teachers' gifts to be shortchanged. My daughter's teacher spent much time teaching her class to play folk music and perform folk dances. To do this, he necessarily reduced time given to the full spectrum of the various art activities normally found in Waldorf schools. My daughter may never play folk music again, or perform the dances she learned, but the experience of learning over several years from a master, of engaging in more than a cursory way in one art, strengthened her in a way for which I will always be grateful.

3. Black

Steiner's remarks about black, in his color lectures, for example, are not represented in his education lectures. And the idea of a prohibition on the use of black, in drawing or in clothing, cannot be found in his education lectures, nor in his color lectures. Steiner himself wore black nearly every day. Children still loved him.

This is not to dispute the quality of black as a color, or the idea that it may not be an appropriate color for young children to use. When teachers remove black, however, leaving white, pink, and brown in the box of crayons, they create a circumstance in which children with pink skin and brown hair, for example, can draw themselves and their families, but children with black hair cannot. Thoughtful teachers could remove all "earth" colors to induce children to draw with the colors of the rainbow, introducing black at the same time that they introduce other such earth colors.

4. Circle Time

Rudolf Steiner never spoke about circle time, and his descriptions of "main lesson" do not include corresponding concepts. "Circle time" is an educational phenomenon of the late 1970s and 1980s, especially in the United Kingdom, in public schools in particular, brought into Waldorf schools by an unknown route. The Great Barrington Rudolf Steiner School library contains a book from 1983, *Everyday Circle Times*, by Liz and Dick Wilmes. It's a fun book, with a faux Peter Max, feel-good cover, lots of pen and ink illustrations, and suggestions for dozens of circle time activities. The school has many other books on circle time, including one celebrating thirty-nine different religious festivals. Not one of these books has a connection to Rudolf Steiner's educational work. A Google search and a search on Amazon.com yield more than 100 "circle time" titles going back to the early 1970s. Few of these references have anything to do with Waldorf education. Clearly, more schools that are not Waldorf schools have circle time than there are Waldorf schools. And it is likely that the form and content of circle time in a Waldorf school is different from elsewhere; like other practices, Waldorf schools adopt and adapt for their own purposes. There's nothing necessarily or inherently wrong with circle time, but to claim circle time as a unique or necessary part of Waldorf school early childhood and elementary schools is clearly incorrect. To believe that it originates in Steiner's work is also incorrect.

5. Consensus

Steiner has little to say about school decision-making and does not use the word consensus or its possible German correlates. When Henry Monges asked Steiner about the process for selecting general secretaries for the Anthroposophical Societies in various countries, Steiner replied:

> This is a further matter which I would not wish to lay down in any way by means of statutes for the various groups all over the world. I can well imagine, for example, that there are national Societies who will most certainly want to employ democratic procedures.

I can also imagine that there will be others who will want to be thoroughly aristocratic in their approach.... Thus I rather assume that the, shall I say, somewhat aristocratic method I have adopted with regard to appointing the Vorstand may well be imitated. In some quarters, however, this method may be regarded as highly undesirable, and in those quarters the democratic method could be used (1990a).

Later, he adds that, because of "mutual recognition,...in practice there will be little difference between democracy and aristocracy....Anyone who is expected to carry out a function must have freedom above all else." These words on choosing Society leaders translate easily to comment on much decision-making in Waldorf schools. "Consensus" is one form of democracy; republican representation is another; direct voter referendum a third; and we can imagine others; and as such, consensus is a valuable concept for making decisions. We should be clear, however, when we adopt this model, that this is a decision we make; we are not following Steiner's commandment. And when others choose, in mutual recognition, a different model, we must acknowledge their right to do so.

Further, it is clear that we have work to do in implementing an understanding of Steiner's work on social health. We acknowledge that teachers have the freedom to carry out their functions as teachers, but we are less clear about the role of school administrators and trustees. To take a hypothetical example, it is clear that teachers must be free to admit those students whom they believe they can teach. There is no consensus involved here. It should be equally clear that another administrative body (a rights administration, perhaps consisting of teachers, administrators, and others) must guarantee the rights of the applicant and her family to participate in a fair process, regardless of the final decision. Here, too, legal and ethical requirements reign, regardless of consensus.

6. Drugs

Steiner discusses the effects of drugs common to his time (caffeine, nicotine, even opium) but not marijuana, LSD, amphetamines, and so on. The spread of the use of these drugs, especially among teenagers, should be a prime concern of Waldorf schools; yet they are hardly better controlled or managed here than they are in other schools. Waldorf schools should be at least as concerned about teen drug use as they are about media exposure in the early grades. Schools have media policies that necessarily extend beyond school hours; imagine the parent of a young child saying, "Well, she wasn't watching TV on school property." The effects of drugs extend beyond the time of their use, and so should school drug policies. Since the 1960s we sometimes find it convenient to believe that teens "will" experiment with drugs. If this is our belief, we will find it to be true. If we choose to combat this view, we may count on some success.

7. Early Childhood Education

Few people know that the first Waldorf school in Stuttgart had a kindergarten for only about six months during Steiner's lifetime; it ceased existence before he died, I believe, because the school needed the space as it grew. Further, Steiner's educational lectures contain much about the development of young children, but little about their actual education. Given his view of child development, it is easy to laud the growth of Waldorf early childhood programs, but their practices (silks, singsong voices, rosy walls) cannot always be said to represent direct indications of Steiner himself. Consequently, we can imagine other forms of early childhood education that appear different but that equally fulfill Steiner's intentions. Howard's essay, referenced above, is a healthy look in this direction.

8. Eight Years of Elementary School

According to Mark Riccio (2002), who has looked into records from Steiner's time, an eight-year elementary school was a state requirement in Germany and Switzerland, and so the eight-year cycle was a compromise; Steiner would have preferred seven. Anyone who has been a class teacher of eighth graders (not that it isn't fantastically rewarding), can appreciate that these students are ready for a different educational form. Knowing this (studying Riccio's work, for example) can inform teaching in upper elementary grades of a Waldorf school.

9. Elementary School Admissions

Between 1930 and today, the age at which students were generally welcomed into first grade in Waldorf schools was delayed six months, from turning six by December first to turning six by June first. Steiner's general description of school-entering age, having to do with losing milk teeth, refers to "the seventh year," which begins on a child's sixth birthday and ends on her seventh (a child's first year occurs from birth until a first birthday). Older children may be easier to manage in first grade, but ninth-grade-age students in an eighth grade class setting can present a real challenge. We live in a world in which an often unquestioned assumption is that "earlier is better"; we do not necessarily need to substitute the contrasting view that "later is always better."

10. Faculty-Run Schools

Steiner simply never said that schools should be "faculty run," and the first school in Stuttgart was not faculty run. Emil Molt footed the bill, and Rudolf Steiner, who was not on the faculty of the school, was the director.

According to Betty Staley, Stewart Easton, a professor and anthroposophist in New York, determined that the "faculty run" method was appropriate and fostered it, in particular, in his students who were interested in anthroposophy (Staley, 1999). Easton's ideas may have originated in England, or they may have been his own interpretation. Steiner described the Waldorf School as "self-administered" (*Eigenrat* or *Selbstverwaltung*), not "faculty run." (Staley, 1998) Literally, these terms mean that schools should take their own advice in self-administration.

Steiner is clear that, in his view, administrators should be active teachers, not state ministers or civil servants, or even retired teachers (1992). Administration is not governance, however, or is not all of it. For Steiner, administration dealt specifically with day-to-day pedagogical operation of the school (pedagogical practice, schedule, calendar) and not necessarily with other governance areas (funding, budget, and legal incorporation in particular). These areas, as they are found in independent schools in the United States today, were hardly conceivable in Germany after World War I. At various times in the life of the Stuttgart school, especially in its first years, various arrangements held sway from time to time. At no time, however, could the first Waldorf school be said to be, or intended to be, faculty run.

I also do not believe it is correct to say that Steiner's role in the first Waldorf school was a unique exception—that he was an initiate and therefore could participate in a way closed to the rest of us. Nothing in his work leads to the conclusion that initiates can transcend rules in this way. The point is not, then, that he included himself as director and participant at faculty meetings as an exception, but that the possibility is open for schools today to include in faculty meetings (or college meetings) those who do not teach at the school but who add value to its community.

Further, U.S. schools have misinterpreted Steiner's remarks about a "college of teachers," or collegium. According to Uta Taylor-Weaver (undated) and to Nancy Parsons Whittaker (2001), the German use of *Collegium* translates as "faculty." The British, they say, see a college as an exclusive group; that was not Steiner's intention. For schools to have a college separate from the faculty, and to have separate weekly meetings for these groups, can foster an exclusivity that Steiner opposed. (See also "Meeting Martyrdom" below.)

11. Festivals

Steiner spoke beautifully, powerfully, repeatedly, and in depth about religious festivals and their meanings. These lectures, however, occur outside the context of his educational lectures. It is not a bad thing that schools participate in annual festivals and rituals as described by Steiner, except in two cases. The first is when these are represented as part and parcel of Waldorf education. They are not; as cultures and traditions change, and as schools are founded in non-Christian nations, it is appropriate that the festivals and rituals celebrated at a school change, too. The second case occurs when schools that are multicultural do not recognize this, and marginalize, say, a Jewish segment of the school population through representations of Christian festivals. It is appropriate to include many different festivals in the school, or to move all festivals outside of school hours, or, as in Austria itself, to leave festivals to the local community, separate from the school. (I am grateful to

Michael D'Aleo for pointing this out following a visit to Austria one December.) I do not mean to confuse festivals with assemblies; Steiner favored periodic assemblies for parents and others at which students could demonstrate what they had learned.

12. Group Meditation

Group meditation, as practiced and modeled by Georg Kühlewind, for example, seems not to have been part of Steiner's repertoire. Steiner's work on meditation makes it clear that this is largely an individual, private practice. It is not wrong for a group or community to practice group meditation, but it should be clear that this choice is not grounded in Steiner's practice or indications. Teachers who balk at group meditation should have their views accommodated in a school community.

13. Holism

Again, a word that cannot be found in Steiner's work. Also, a word that requires work to understand. A materialist—like James Lovelock, inventor of the computer models that are termed the Gaia hypothesis—can be a holist, as can someone who denies the existence of the material world. Holism exists in many forms. Using the word colloquially, on the other hand, can drain it of meaning.

14. Low Academic Standards

Steiner himself had a doctorate, no mean feat in nineteenth century Germany. A bracing quotation cuts to the quick:

The aim of Waldorf education is to arrange all of the teaching so that within the shortest possible time the maximum amount of material can be presented to students by the simplest possible means. [This is one of just half a dozen instances of Steiner's use of the phrase "Waldorf education." In German, the phrase is *Waldorfschulpaedagogik*, literally, "the pedagogy used in the Waldorf School."] (2003).

Schools can work harder to implement "soul economy," and to demonstrate to parents and communities that there is no compromise between a good academic education and a Waldorf school education. This will not mean teaching more material sooner; chasing the local independent day school; or aiming for high scores on a standardized test; but teaching more deeply and more consciously.

15. Math Gnomes

As Christine Cox demonstrates in her M.S.Ed. thesis (2006), math gnomes and other imaginative, anthropomorphic versions of arithmetic operations such as King Plus actually work against Steiner's understanding of math teaching. Math, akin to other spiritual activities, which we may picture as belonging to Plato's eternal "intelligible" or ideal realm, needs to be brought to earth through practical, real-world problems. Steiner advocates beginning to teach arithmetic with the operation of division by bringing a pile of pieces of paper or beans into the classroom (2000, 7).

Although math gnomes were the invention of Dorothy Harrer (based on verses by Margaret Peckham, both of them celebrated Waldorf school class teachers), the wisdom of Steiner and his student Hermann von Baravalle, suggest that we should liberate math gnomes and other such beings from Waldorf school curricula. Math teaching should be imaginative, but not fantastic. Students exercise precise imagination in math by entering clearly into the concepts of their work. Imagination should aid this process, not distract from it, as I fear math gnomes do.

16. Meeting Martyrdom

The first Waldorf school had nearly 800 pupils and a commensurate number of teachers in its first few years of existence; yet it had only one faculty meeting per week. There was no inner circle, no separate College or Council, although there was an "extended faculty." It included those we might call subcontractors today; they taught at the school but were not necessarily committed to its mission. Most independent Waldorf schools today have separate faculty and college or council meetings, in addition to "school" meetings of the early childhood, elementary school, or high school faculties. This is not to mention the plethora of board and school committee meetings that dedicated teachers attend. Eugene Schwartz has recommended that schools cut in half the number of meetings they hold. Schools with fewer meetings demonstrate greater trust in the work of the faculty and staff, and enjoy the fruits of these individuals' initiatives.

17. Non-Competitive Games

Again, not necessarily a bad thing, but not based clearly on Steiner's work. Non-competitive games are more likely an outgrowth of the counterculture of the 1960s and 1970s than a clearly anthroposophic point of view. Competition is a part of the healthy function of the spiritual sphere of the threefold social organism, and could find its reflection in healthy competition in schools.

18. Notebooks, Main Lesson Books, Good Books

My suspicion is that notebooks—illustrated, decorated exercise books and textbooks—as found in Waldorf schools are part of German education in the 1920s and not unique to Waldorf schools. Steiner found the readers and textbooks of his age execrable and spoke against their deadening influence. This injunction, however, does not necessarily translate into a dictum to produce illustrated manuals for every main lesson, especially when students may spend hours decorating the borders of pages or slavishly copying a teacher's notes. Similarly, it is difficult to know what Steiner would say about contemporary textbooks, including those written by Waldorf school teachers, which come in an increasingly broad variety.

19. Pedagogical Stories

Steiner is clear that nature and the world around us provide the raw material for all necessary "pedagogical stories." Teachers do not have to include such characters as cute elementals or anthropomorphic frogs in order to create interest in the lessons they aim to impart through such stories; children see right through these concoctions. Instead, teachers can find the objective truth that they wish to impart in the truth of the world around them. Such an approach to storytelling brings us closer to Barfield's "final participation," wherein the inner truth of our metaphors and the truth of the world around us become one.

20. State Control of Schools

The United States has always enjoyed greater local control of schools (through taxes, school boards, and local governments suspicious of centralized control) than any other modern nation. We do not have federal or state school inspectors, as Germany did in Steiner's time; and schools belong to voluntary accrediting organizations. To turn away from engagement with local schools, public or independent, causes Waldorf schools to appear cloistered and out of the mainstream. Why not join with other independent schools, as the Rudolf Steiner School in New York did in the 1930s, to promote good education for more children? Why not forge alliances with local public schools to share knowledge and resources, and to combat the encroachment of such measures as "No Child Left Behind," which few public school teachers or administrators endorse?

21. Trademark of "Waldorf" and "Steiner"

The Association of Waldorf Schools of North America has trademarked Rudolf Steiner's name and the name "Waldorf" as these apply to school names:

> Waldorf is a trademark name in the United States and is reserved for independent schools that meet the membership standards established by AWSNA. Only schools that have been accepted as Sponsored or Full Members of AWSNA may represent themselves as Waldorf schools or use the words "Waldorf" or "Rudolf Steiner" in their names or subtitles. (2005)

The value of a trademark on merchandise such as crayons or pencils or dolls is clear, as is the value of a professional association; but Steiner is mum on the question of the protection or trademark, for schools, of his name, or the name "Waldorf." Another point of view might be that anyone courageous enough to pursue education along these lines might be allowed to use these names; that the dangers of standardization and dogma are greater than or outweigh the danger of dilution or misrepresentation. Despite recent efforts by AWSNA to clarify the issue, it is difficult to understand how a fledgling or "new initiative" [Waldorf] school could be expected to grow to the point of sustainability, at which time AWSNA would recognize it and allow it to use Steiner's name or the term "Waldorf" in its name. The dozen or so schools that pre-existed AWSNA between 1928 and 1980, the schools that jointly created AWSNA, did not face this hurdle in their own development.

22. Waldorf dolls

I remember my wife, Janis, knitting until 2 a.m. one Christmas morning in order to complete a doll for our son, and I remember how he treasured his "Gnome Prince" for years. Janis spent many dollars and many hours creating a beautiful gift for our son. But we miss the point if we believe he treasured the natural materials, the expense, or the time it took to create his doll. In *The Education of the Child*, Steiner advocates tying knots in a handkerchief and adding inkblots to make a doll (1996a). This is a far cry from the expensive, natural material kits—available from Martha Stewart, among others—from which, often, we painstakingly produce our Waldorf dolls. Such costs, materials, and time are a luxury, not one easily found in post-World War I Germany, I would guess. And Waldorf education is clearly intended to be not only for the wealthy.

Courage and Imagination

When we are blinded by the beautiful trappings of an education we treasure, we are in danger of stepping into the modern "sin of literalness" (Barfield, 1998). We are then, regardless of professed beliefs or values, edging close to a kind of fundamentalism based on a materialism that we say we wish to overcome.

It is easy to tell ourselves not to be blind, harder to suggest a cure. As Owen Barfield put it, unlearning a habit of thought is as difficult as unlearning how to ride a bicycle (1979). We may begin, however, by enlarging our relationship with Steiner's work. We may do this by hewing more closely to what he actually said—and not to what he didn't say—and having the courage to imagine more fully what this might mean.

9. WHAT MAKES WALDORF, WALDORF?

So what is essential to the practices and understandings of Waldorf schools and Waldorf school teachers? If Rudolf Steiner's work on teaching and learning is not to be seen partially, inaccurately, or superficially, how can it be seen? Can we see Waldorf education whole?

The Checklist Test

We could begin by creating a checklist of all the things Steiner said about teaching and learning. I suggest this as a thought experiment only, somewhat tongue-in-cheek. I hope not to see a future publication entitled, *The Waldorf Teacher's Checklist of Everything Rudolf Steiner Had to Say about Teaching and Learning.* The list would include items that deal with the mundane, the sublime, and everything in between—discipline and math teaching, destiny, and temperament. If we create and examine such a list, I believe, we would recognize that we are "babes in the woods" when it comes to actually doing Waldorf education. We are generally not seers. Our spiritual development may be strong in many ways but it is infantile in others.

It may be many years, many generations, before we can begin to approach Steiner as an equal, and do more than begin to implement education the way he envisaged it. By way of analogy, consider Aristotle's work on gravity. This was accepted, unquestioned, for nearly 2000 years, until Galileo, avatar of a consciousness beyond Aristotle's, was able to meet gravity on new terms, and demonstrate ways in which Aristotle's thinking was incorrect. Who today can do the same for

Steiner? More importantly, who today can equal or even approach Steiner in insight and understanding?

Which items on our list are essential and which may be altered or dispensed with? Our rudimentary understanding of Waldorf education may fail us. One item looks much like another. How else may we proceed?

The Tin Shack Test

Another thought experiment by which to test what is essential in Steiner's view of teaching and learning is what I call the Tin Shack Test. Clearly, Waldorf education is compromised if it exists solely for the benefit of the few wealthy families that can afford private school tuition. It must be possible to practice education in a fruitful and health-giving way, even if our school building is a tin shack and we have no money for supplies. Any quality or characteristic or practice of teaching and learning that cannot find itself in the tin shack—or the shade of a tree, for example—is probably not essential.

By "wealthy," I should say, I mean almost all of us. Half the world lives on the equivalent of a dollar or two per day. Those of us fortunate enough to have hot and cold running water, a refrigerator, and an automobile should consider ourselves to be among the wealthiest persons ever to walk the planet. In the ancient world, the number of servants or slaves necessary to maintain us in such luxury would have been in the hundreds.

The Essence of Essence

The word that Steiner most frequently used to describe what I am talking about is the German noun *Wesen*, which translates as "being," as in "human being." The German is less concrete than its English counterpart, however, and may also be translated as "nature," as in Socrates' "medicine has to define the nature of the body." And it may further be translated as "essence," as in Zoolander's "moisture is the essence of wetness." When Steiner uses the word *Wesen*, we mistake ourselves in English if our minds leap to a concept of corporeality, too often associated in English with the word "being." The essence of being, we may say, is of an immaterial nature.

I am aware, however, of a large literature, including especially Fuchs (2001), that limns the dangers of thinking that approaches essentials, giving rise to a new form of prejudice, "essentialism." I take the central argument here to be that so often in history what we have believed contained some essential quality—whiteness or maleness, for example—turned out later on, or on careful inspection, not to. Much of the world that seems so given and so real is, in fact, contingent, or at least created, situational, and symbolic; and is likely to change from time to time and context to context. So we must approach "Waldorfness" with great care, ready to find that it's not what we thought it was, and may not be anything at all.

As Samuel Taylor Coleridge said, however, and as so many have quoted, we can distinguish in the mind what we cannot divide in the world (1969-present). My aim here is to distinguish what for Waldorf teachers is central to their understanding of what we do, recognizing that this may change over time, or with changing contexts. I am not burrowing into the center of a planet to find its core; I am examining a box of artifacts, if you will, to discover those that (in my estimation) better reveal the unique qualities of the person to whom it belongs.

Imagining the Best

What, then, is essential to teaching and learning, according to Steiner's work, according to his images of human beings and the world? One method for approaching the question of the core of what we call Waldorf education is to imagine what we could not do without, in a broad and durable sense. Which aspects of our work, if we were forbidden to implement them, might lead us to close our doors, or declare that we could no longer call ourselves Waldorf teachers or a Waldorf school?

I will posit, hesitantly, that there are five categories, each of which is taken to be essential to what we do in Waldorf schools. Readers will note that any teacher, any school, could adopt these practices and understandings. I will let others determine at what point, level, or degree of commitment a person becomes a Waldorf teacher, a school becomes a Waldorf school. My own view is that anyone courageous enough to want to work with Steiner's ideas on education deserves our support and admiration, regardless of setting or circumstance.

I say "hesitantly" because I may well have the number wrong. Biologists who count species, for example, may be termed "lumpers" (those who overlook minor differences in favor of underlying sameness) or "splitters" (those who see relatively minor differences as significant). I attempt neither a lumper nor a splitter to be, and I acknowledge that I may be overlooking something important, a sixth or seventh essential; or I may be including too many separating characteristics that would better be combined. I welcome correction.

Fortunately, these five aspects of education may be seen as facets of one encompassing whole. While the myths of Waldorf education multiply beyond counting, the essentials tend toward one. I end by considering characteristics of this whole.

Five Gifts

One way to picture the five essentials is to see them as gifts that Waldorf school teachers give their graduates; I mean primarily high school graduates. Lower school parents and graduates will recognize these gifts, but they will also recognize that none comes fully to fruition by the end of eighth grade.

I previously quoted Peter Curran on what he saw as the four "essentials...without which no school (by whatever name) is a Waldorf School and with which any school is a Waldorf School." His essentials are essentially the same as the first four gifts I describe below, I believe; and are noteworthy in omitting consideration of the last, social health. I believe this omission is a symptom of Curran's generation; it is really only in the last couple of decades, in the United States, at least, that a serious conversation about the "social mission" of Waldorf education has been reinvigorated. Talk of a social mission was somewhat forgotten, we may posit, during the tension of the Cold War. Consideration of that hypothesis here, however, would take us too far afield.

1. Ideas and Ideals

The first gift is a source of ideas and ideals. Waldorf education does not provide beliefs, ideology, culture, or worldview, although it necessarily manifests a collection of cultures and can devolve into ideology.

(The "Waldorf worldview," at least in its mundane expression, is an expression of time and place, and is not essential. Countercultural or alternative education only came into being in the 1960s, for example.) Belief, knowledge, and worldview may be "about" spiritual matters, but they should not be mistaken for them. An intellectual understanding of Waldorf education does not make a teacher, and highly gifted teachers may be poor at discussing what they do and how they do it.

What teachers provide, more important than any knowledge about a way of life or a worldview, is a pathway or method for discovering these ideas and ideals, should a student wish later in life to pursue them. Choosing this path, following it, and putting into practice the results of such a journey involve human freedom, moral imagination, ethical individualism; or call it what you will.

As teachers, all we can give of value with regard to spiritual realities is a path that can be followed or retraced. In geometry, I can show how the steps of a proof lead to a logical conclusion, but you must take that final intuitive leap yourself. If you do not "see" that these steps constitute a proof, all I can do as a teacher is retrace the path, perhaps using different language or different symbols, in order to help you again to the brink of intuitive understanding. Anthroposophically-gained knowledge of the world, given to us in Steiner's books and lectures, for example, can provide stepping stones akin to the statements in a geometric proof. They attain meaning, however, only as we use them to focus our attention, to trace and retrace a path to the spirit, to meaning, and to understanding.

This first point encompasses Steiner's work in education and also the anthroposophic method and knowledge that underlies it (understandings of destiny, reincarnation, the place of human beings in the cosmos and in evolution, and so on). To treat these understandings as part of an ideology or worldview is to belittle them, to turn them into a religion. If they are true, they are true for all people and they are facts about the world; they are evidence of a science and a scientific method.

If the freedom to teach toward this path of understanding were denied, a teacher would have to feel that she could no longer teach as a "Waldorf" teacher. In this regard, I will add for more philosophical readers that I see Steiner's work primarily as work in method, and that considerations of epistemology or ontology arise secondarily to this focus on method.

2. Development

> In the future, all instruction must be built upon psychology developed from an anthroposophical understanding of the world. (Steiner, 1996b, 49)

> What lives in human beings tends toward metamorphosis. If you can bring it about that the children have concepts of respect and honoring, concepts of all that we can call, in an all encompassing sense, a prayerful attitude, then such thoughts will be living in children permeated with a prayerful attitude, and will remain into old age. In old age, these concepts will be transformed into a capacity to bless and to give others the results of a prayerful attitude. (155)

> You must be a good friend of natural development. (180)

Second, teachers address their students as developing human beings, beings who transform themselves unconsciously in youth and later become uniquely capable of self-transformation. In nature, metamorphoses and transformations are primarily visible. We can see a plant grow from shoot to leaves to flower, each stage presenting unforeseen changes of form. No one looking at a caterpillar for the first time would guess that it would soon be a butterfly. In human life, especially after childhood, however, transformation and development are not so readily visible.

Waldorf teachers seek patterns in human development, and they also seek to be sensitive to the unique development of each student. They may fruitfully seek a common language with developmental psychologists. If a teacher in a Waldorf school were prohibited from addressing his students according to a developmentally appropriate model, he might well feel he could no longer call himself a Waldorf teacher. The question of development leads naturally to the question of the relationship of Rudolf Steiner's concepts of development to those of Jean Piaget.

In the course of my research on the history of Waldorf schools in the United States many people with whom I spoke, admissions directors and teachers among them, casually compared Steiner's ideas on the development of children in stages with the developmental research of Piaget. My initial reactions were that this comparison must be meant allegorically and that it wouldn't bear scrutiny. Steiner and Piaget's reputations were simply too dissimilar; what could the seer and the scientist have in common? The intention, it seemed, was to lend Piaget's weight as a scientist to Steiner's less familiar reputation as an educator. Comparing the two has not changed my suspicions regarding the intentions behind the comparison, but it has thrown some light on the intersection of, for education, arguably the two most important developmentalists of the twentieth century. The ways in which Steiner and Piaget's ideas on child development are similar, and dissimilar, were not what I had expected.

Piaget on Education

Ignoring the many inferences regarding education that may be drawn from Piaget's research, he wrote surprisingly little on education. Only one essay, begun in 1935 and completed in 1965(!), examines education in general, including the application of Piaget's research to education. The essay is a curious hodge-podge of explanation, correction, and opinion. Called "Science of Education and the Psychology of the Child" (1935 and 1965), it begins by examining the psychological foundations of "new methods" in education, and concludes that "active" learning is superior to "passive" learning. It contains, however, the warning that "memory, passive obedience, imitation of the adult, and the receptive factors in general are as natural to the child as spontaneous activity" (696). This fine distinction between "passive" and "receptive" shows Piaget's attention to children's inner worlds.

Piaget goes on to bemoan the degree to which education professionals in general have not applied to teaching what is known of child development. He remarks that many profound education reformers were philosophers or doctors, not pedagogues, Comenius, Rousseau, Froebel, Dewey, and Montessori among them. And their thinking and research has not become the foundation for a science of education:

The general problem is to understand why the vast army of educators now laboring throughout the entire world with such devotion and, in general, with such competence does not engender an elite of researchers capable of making pedagogy into a discipline, at once scientific and alive, that could take its rightful place among all those

other applied disciplines that draw upon both art and science...
(699)

Much of the rest of the essay gives Piaget's opinions on the teaching
of mathematics, philosophy, and the humanities. The essay concludes
with a look at four categories of teaching methods: the receptive, the
active, the intuitive, and the programmed. (By "intuitive," Piaget means
a method that asks the student to infer an educational lesson from an
external representation; manipulatives, filmstrips, and pottery would
each be intuitive by Piaget's definition. For Piaget, the meaning of intuitive is literal and technical, not transcendental.) The last category, the
programmed, includes especially early use of computers in the classroom, and has been fostered in the United States especially by Piaget's
pupil, Seymour Papert (see Papert, 1980). Piaget notes that many people confuse active and intuitive methods because they take activity too
literally, forgetting or ignoring inner, mental activity.

Ginsburg on Steiner and Piaget

Despite the number of times I have heard Steiner and Piaget mentioned in one breath, I am aware of only one published consideration
of their work. This is a brief but excellent article by Iona Ginsburg
(1982) that compares the stages of child development as conceptualized
by Rudolf Steiner and by Jean Piaget. She correlates Piaget's stages of
cognitive development (sensori-motor, concrete operations, and formal
operations), with Steiner's descriptions of human development (imitative, imaginative, and intellectual phases). A note on stages: Piaget is clear
regarding his definition of "stage," while Steiner uses a less technical
vocabulary. For development to occur according to a change from one
stage to another, according to Piaget, the order of succession may not
vary; developed characteristics must be cumulative; periods of change
must be followed by periods of equilibrium; and so on (Piaget, 1955).
These requirements apply, too, to Steiner's descriptions of development.
Growth alone, as simple accumulation, is not developmental. "Phases"
that come and go often do not meet the criteria for stage development.
"Age appropriate" learning or behavior may or may not occur within
the context of stage development. Stage development is at once more

rigorous and more global than common understandings of maturation. Stage development provides evidence of "metamorphosis," a change in form that signals a concurrent change in quality; the physical and physiological changes of puberty are accompanied by emotional and intellectual changes, and vice versa.

Among Ginsburg's concerns, shared with Piaget himself, is the degree to which Piaget's work, despite its apparent implications for education, has not been applied to classroom practice. She locates this lack in that Piaget's research "leaves out vivid and vital aspects of the child's total development—feeling, attachment, impulse, fantasy, and their impact on cognition itself" (328). Because Steiner focused on "the totality of development" (329), Ginsburg believes his work, despite its lack of conventional scientific rigor, has had greater success in influencing classroom practice.

In comparing Piaget and Steiner's descriptions of stage development, Ginsburg is more specific with regard to ages than either Steiner or Piaget. Steiner (1965 and many other places) refers to a transformation "about age seven" (20), more accurately associated with the loss of milk teeth, a process that often takes more than a year and can begin at age five, or be prolonged well past age seven. Similarly, Piaget (1955) is at pains to emphasize "not the timing, but the order of succession [of acquisition]" in stage development. Chronology, he writes, "is extremely variable; it depends on the previous experience of the individuals, and not only on their maturation, and it depends especially on the social milieu that can accelerate or retard the appearance of a stage, or even prevent its appearance" (815). Steiner tacitly acknowledges this characteristic of a stage, too. While many Waldorf teachers speak of Steiner's stages as if they possessed some concrete reality, Steiner acknowledged not only their relevance to a specific cultural here-and-now, but also their variation based on both spiritual and physiological variations among people (see, for example, *Curative Education*, 1972). The point of Steiner's descriptions was not to normalize a child's place in a class, which is a constant danger of a developmental point of view, regardless of the developmentalist (see Morss, 1995). Steiner's point was to provide insight for better teaching. ("Normalizing" is the process of comparing one child to others with regard to some characteristic that is [or is thought to] be distributed normally—that is, according to a bell curve—throughout the population of all children. The danger when we do this is that we lose sight of the unique individual in our attempt to say something general about all children; we treat a human being as a statistic.)

Ginsburg recognizes that

> Many of the contrasts [between Steiner and Piaget] are based on profound differences in frame of reference and worldview. Piaget, who was not a teacher, focused single-mindedly on the development of the structures of cognition in children, from the perspective of a scientist who studied the changes with age and the growth of the capacity to know. Steiner and the education based on his insights have a view of the stages of child development based largely on intuition, which encompasses awareness of the impact of feeling, fantasy [almost certainly a British mistranslation of what is meant by "imagination"], form, color, and human relatedness in cognitive development.

Five Similarities

While I agree with Ginsburg's recognition of the differences between Steiner and Piaget, I also believe that there are similarities, which she has overlooked. I will examine four of these points below and quote from Steiner's early pamphlet, *The Education of the Child in the Light of Anthroposophy* (1965). Readers familiar with Steiner's work will recognize that he made similar points in dozens of other lectures and writings. More to the point, *The Education of the Child* was actually written by Steiner, not transcribed from the shorthand notes of a lecture, and can therefore be held to be more precisely what he intended to say.

First, both Steiner and Piaget recognize the importance of imitation in the development of children. Steiner writes, "There are two magic words that indicate how the child enters into relations with his environment. They are: Imitation and Example... For no age in life is this more true than for the first stage of childhood, before the change of teeth... The child... does not learn by instruction or admonition, but by imitation" (24-25). Piaget (1962) regards "imitation as the process that ensures the transition from sensori-motor intelligence to representative imagery" (509). That is to say, for example, that it is through imitation that an infant learns to speak. Further, Piaget (1966) describes the "mental image" as an "internalized imitation" (490). This could be Steiner's language as well.

Second, both Steiner and Piaget recognize the importance of symbolic understanding. Steiner writes, "It is essential that the secrets of nature, the laws of life, be taught to the boy or girl, not in dry intellectual concepts, but as far as possible in symbols" (33). Piaget writes, for example, that "Symbolic play is the apogee of children's play" (492).

Third, Piaget's well-known developmental path from assimilation to equilibrium is mirrored, I believe, in Steiner's description of the process by which memories become concepts. "It is necessary for man not only to remember what he understands, but to understand what he already knows—that is to say, what he has acquired by memory in the way the child acquires language... First there must be [for example] the assimilation of historical events through the memory, then the grasping of them in intellectual concepts" (39). Not all memory-to-concept shifts achieve the status of Piagetian equilibrium, clearly; but as each of Steiner's stages is achieved, the *quality* of concepts may be said to alter significantly enough to equate with Piaget's description. Specifically, as Steiner describes, concepts in early life grow from activity engendered through imitation and example; later, they grow from feeling-imbued imagination and appropriate authority; and only then from a rational and relatively abstract understanding.

Last, both Steiner and Piaget developed corresponding "threefold" views of human psychology. Steiner described "the several faculties of the soul—thinking, feeling, and willing" (1965, 41), while Piaget often described "subsystems" of "intellect," "affect," and "activity" (see 1966, 492, for example).

The central or overarching point of agreement, however, is that both Piaget and Steiner found children intrinsically interesting in themselves, and valued children's perception and experience on their own terms. Neither man forwarded a utilitarian nor a "Whig" version of childhood (that is, one that is based on expectations of a known but yet-to-emerge adulthood).

A Big Difference

Steiner and Piaget's use of language differ enormously, however, in *connotation*. When Piaget uses a phrase like "mental image" (1963) or a

word like "imitation" (1962), he is using the terms to designate gener-
alizations based on controlled observations in his life and in his labora-
tory. When Steiner uses the same terms, he is using them as indications
of concepts that, like onions, have layers, and may be understood at
once, for example, on the generic level on which Piaget operates; and
also on potentially more profound levels. Both men were empiricists,
but they would clearly have disagreed on the limits of empiricism. (I
do not believe it is fair to say, as Ginsburg does, that Steiner and Piaget
differed in worldview. It is not possible to intuit from Piaget's careful
scientific writings what his actual worldview may have been.)

It is tempting to say that Piaget's results, more conventionally scientific and more generic than Steiner's, could be subsumed or swallowed
whole by Steiner's more inclusive, comprehensive view or experience.
This does a disservice to both men, however, in that Steiner's point was
often to transcend the generic (see, for example, Bortoft, 1996, especially "Modes of Consciousness," 61-68). Piaget, by contrast, aimed to
"make of epistemology an experimental discipline as well as a theoretical one" (1995, xi-xii). Both Steiner and Piaget foreswore theorizing as
an end in itself. Both believed powerfully in the value of experience.
Experience, for Steiner, however, expands as faculties of perception and
conception evolve, and is, at root, imaginative and unbounded. Experience, for Piaget, is given through relatively fixed relationships of sense
organs to mind, and within these limits, may be explored through controlled study.

3. Three Kinds of Knowing

> Whenever you want to suitably consider the human being from
> any particular standpoint, you must always return to the three parts
> of the human soul—that is, to cognition that occurs in thinking, to
> feeling, and to willing. (Steiner, 1996b, 106)

Accumulating knowledge is like building a collection, right? Each
piece in the collection is much like any other. A fact about astronomy
is much like a fact about history or writing technique or piano playing
or wine tasting or empathetic listening. A degree of certainty or truth
adheres to it or is apparent in it, and we accept it for our stockpile of

things that we know, which we hope is growing. It can be digitized and stored in a computer and shared online.

Well, no. Knowledge is not singular. Knowing the names of stars is not like knowing how to play the piano, or like knowing how to offer solace to someone in pain. Like intelligence, which we used to believe was one thing (measured on an IQ test, for example), but is now seen as a multi-faceted collection of human faculties, at least; knowledge comes in different forms. We can know in different ways. Waldorf and Steiner schools emphasize in particular three ways of knowing, the conscious development of each corresponding roughly with preschool, elementary school, and high school.

Michael Polanyi called a first kind of knowing "tacit knowing," knowing "more than we can say" (1966). Clearly, infants—those without voices, as the term itself suggests—know more than they can say. We can know how to cut a carrot, or the taste of the soup it makes, or how to play the viola, or how to solve a problem in geometry. We can describe these things in language, but the value, meaning, and even the truth of these activities—cutting, tasting, playing, solving—does not translate into language. These become apparent only when we learn to do these things ourselves. Without the experience of doing, knowing often has little meaning.

You could write a manual describing what you do, as nurse, stockbroker, or artist; but if you had to train someone to replace you, would you rather hand off instructions, or offer an apprenticeship, some doing? Read a book on building a stone wall, and then claim that you know how to build one. Your aches and calluses will tell you another story. We learn much and know much through doing, and doing often precedes and informs our knowing. Hence, in Waldorf schools, the importance of "doing" in preschool, before we emphasize other forms of knowing.

A second kind of knowing is aesthetic knowing. Its value is apparent in contrast to our concept of something that is anesthetic, or numbing. Aesthetic knowing is alive, awake, and sensitive. It is knowing in heart and gut (yes, the brain plays its role, but we experience our feelings in our hearts and lungs and guts). It is intuitive ("taught from within"). It is a form of knowing especially valuable for artists, musicians, clinical psychologists, theoretical physicists, and even advertising copywriters. It is a form of knowing that connects us powerfully to the world. And it develops in children most readily when they have separated from their

parents and begun to comprehend the world around them for themselves. Hence, in Waldorf schools, the importance of beauty and feeling
in the elementary school.

A third kind of knowing is knowing through thinking. By thinking,
however, I mean a particular kind of thinking that attempts to "swim
upstream," in Henri Bortoft's phrase, reversing fragmentation, categori-
zation, and specialization in order to recover wholeness (1996). Thinking
logically with given postulates, thinking algorithmically, is "downstream"
thinking, the outcome determined by the input. It is powerful but dead,
inherited from the creative insight of others. Recognizing the validity
of postulates different from convention, however, involves insight of our
own. This synthetic, living thinking can encompass or embrace analysis,
logic, and critical thinking. But it seeks to go beyond them to recover or
reach the origin of creative thought and imagination. And it develops in
students who are wrestling not so much with the world around them as
with their own identities in that world. Hence, in Waldorf schools, the
importance in high school of the development of thinking.

These three ways of knowing are cumulative and integrative. We do
not leave one for the next, but build on what comes before. As adults,
our thinking is enriched if we also know how to do and to feel. All
three forms of knowing are present earlier, too—small children learning to walk and talk (two of the most important forms of doing) can
also feel and think. But by emphasizing one way of knowing at the
appropriate time, allowing other ways to develop simultaneously but
sleepily, we work in accordance with children's growth away from their
parents and into the world and themselves. We know in our hands, in
our hearts, and in our heads. We know goodness, beauty, and truth. The
more ways we know, the more value we find in life, and the more value
we bring to those around us and to whatever we are called to do.

Again, this third point may belong to a subset of the first. Anyone
treading a path of understanding will recognize that there are different
modes of existence and ways of knowing.

4. Social Health

Fourth, a school can provide profound examples and guidelines
for a healthy life with other people. If they choose to, Waldorf school

graduates know how to live with others in brotherhood and sisterhood, in solidarity. They know how to be the appropriate equal of any man or any woman. And they know where their individual freedom lies, the sort of freedom that laws and conventions cannot touch. Steiner's description of a healthy "threefold" social organism can be seen as a common-sense description of reality (not a utopian vision that does not and will not exist) by students who have lived through years in a Waldorf school.

This point, too, derives from the first. Who, on a spiritual path, would not strive to bring into existence an ever-healthier social world?

5. Reverence and the World

Fifth, students receive a reverence for life and for the world; a concern for the environment, however defined. I mention this last and say the least about it here because as a society we have probably embraced this gift more fully in the past fifty years than we have the others. Peace education, environmental and ecological education, outdoor action programs, and other forms of holistic education may find fellow travelers in Waldorf teachers here.

Only in Waldorf?

Waldorf school curricula and methods lend themselves to an education in all of these five areas. Various schools may struggle at times with one or another. Various teachers evince strengths in particular directions. Taken together, however, these cover the ground, I believe, of what is essential to Waldorf education. It should be clear, then, that any school, any teachers can give these gifts. But the sad truth is that in our world today only in Waldorf schools can you consistently find teachers united in common purpose to strive to give their students fully and consistently what I have outlined here.

The Big One

While the trappings of Waldorf education multiply beyond counting, the essentials, few in number, perhaps five, perhaps more or fewer, cohere toward one. Another approach to the essential nature of Waldorf education deserves mention. If my first five points present a chorus of gifts, this last image is a single, sounding gong. At the center of any method of teaching must reside an image of the human being who is learning and being taught, the human being becoming ever more human.

Previously, human beings were seen as born in original sin and, therefore, needing to be saved (Jonathan Edwards). Or they were seen as growing healthfully in a metaphorical garden, inadvertently damaged or corrupted by the unhealthful influence of imperfect civilization (Jean Jacques Rousseau). Or as "blank slates" on which society, civilization, and teachers could write (John Locke). Or as citizens to be educated for participation in a democratic government (Thomas Jefferson); amoral immigrants to be moralized (Horace Mann); future contributing members of a community (John Dewey); or more recently, as biological systems that support brains that need to be programmed (Seymour Papert).

A more profound image of a human being arises if we consider that we are created in a creator's image. I take this to mean not that God has ten fingers and ten toes; but that, like our creator, we are creative. An education that places creativity at its core, and that derives its methods from this understanding of imagination not as an accessory or enhancement to an academic education, but as the ground from which all knowledge springs, may be called Waldorf education.

What is Creativity?

The meaning of creativity, however, is not clear. What does it mean to be creative? Does it mean a practice of art—and not science—without standards, objectivity, or rigor? Pursued this way, creativity is seen as a healthful hiatus from more important pursuits, a necessary venting before returning to the real business of life. Or is creativity a heaven-opening moment of insight, bestowed on some and not on others, "eurekas" and "ah-hahs" as gifts of divine grace? Pursued this way, it is, like the works that creative persons produce, unavailable for scientific study or human understanding.

Such views do not hold up to scrutiny.

History is replete with descriptions of moments of insight, from Archimedes on down, but we should not forget who the persons are who receive these insights. Mathematical truths may be raining down on you and me this moment; but, without rigorous training, hard work, a developed understanding of symbolic systems, and who knows what else, we are incapable of perceiving them.

Research in creativity by such eminent psychologists as Piaget's pupil, Howard Gruber, demonstrates creativity to be something else altogether. For Gruber, whose seminal work was a study of Charles Darwin (*Darwin on Man*), creativity is a capacity of scientists as much as of artists. It results in novelty, new creations, and is the result of unique, creative human efforts. To honor the uniqueness of creative acts, Gruber questioned even such thoughtful research as the "multiple intelligence" work of Howard Gardner, and championed the case study method, the study of creativity person by person. (Gruber was not opposed to multiple intelligence theory, he just didn't think it resulted in a description of creativity.)

This is not to say, however, that creativity cannot be studied scientifically. The lives of creative persons, as Gruber showed, have many points in common (1989).

- They undergo periods of apprenticeship.
- They work hard to achieve insight, and work hard after insight, expressing and testing it, putting it in a form that others can understand.
- They live lives in a "network of enterprise," which are mutually supporting endeavors and experiences that contribute to creative work. Without Darwin's avocational interest in geology, for instance, it is possible that he might not have achieved his insights into the evolution of living species.
- The work and lives of creative persons evolve, as well, demonstrating a (unique) pattern that can be understood and retraced by others.
- And, in order to make sense of their work, creative persons develop and employ "images of wide scope" or "ensembles of metaphor." Darwin wrestled with the image we now know as the "tree" that showed the evolution of life, working through several branching images, including a coral (1981).

Gruber wondered to the end whether or not everyone is creative (Personal communication, 1998). He chose to study eminent artists and scientists, and sometimes expressed the view that only a few persons are actually creative; the rest of us simply live our lives. But he also believed in the unity of human experience, and wondered what it might mean to say that everyone is creative in some way. Certainly the elements of his studies may be applied to the review—or conduct—of any life.

Creativity, Morality, and Freedom

Gruber also recognized the connection between creativity and morality:

> Our conceptions of creativity and morality are intertwined in a number of ways.... At once we see that the indispensable middle term between creativity and morality is freedom. We can hardly speak of a moral act if the actor has no choice. Creative work also requires inner freedom.... Creative work must be in some ways kindred to the world, if not the world as it is, then the world as it will or might be. It flows out of that world and it flows back into it. Thus the creative person, to carry out the responsibility to self, the responsibility for inner integrity, must also in some way be responsive to the world. (1989, 280-281)

Seen in this way, it seems clear that what Steiner called "ethical individualism" and "moral imagination" contribute to a conversation about creativity: "Freedom of action is thinkable only from the standpoint of ethical individualism" (1995, 154). And: "Free spirits need *moral imagination* to realize their ideas and make them effective. Moral imagination is the source of a free spirit's actions. Therefore, only people who have moral imagination are really morally productive" (1995, 182).

Contemplation

Finally, it's worth opening a topic with which some readers may wish I had started this section: meditation, active thinking, or contemplative spiritual exercises. Although I have just spent some ink writing about creativity, freedom, and morality, I could as well have devoted the space to meditation.

The link among these is insight. What does a teacher need, what does creativity require, what deserts the unfree, and if morality is seen as something developed within each individual within a specific context (and not as something imposed according to an external code), what is the source of morality? Insight.

What is the path to insight? It begins in hard work, apprenticeship, and so on; it has all the hallmarks of the work of a creative person. And it also requires hard, active thinking in Barfield's sense; real contemplation, or meditation in the sense in which Steiner often spoke of it. The methods of Waldorf education multiply; but their source, initially in Steiner, may be found since then in each teacher who seeks insight through contemplation, active thinking, or meditation.

It's Not All About Steiner

In arguing against one sort of fundamentalism (the sort that would mistake and assert superficial characteristics and techniques of Waldorf education for an essence), some readers may believe I am leaning toward another fundamentalism—"if it's not in Steiner's work, it's not Waldorf education." This is not the case. I am fully aware that many valuable characteristics of and practices in Waldorf schools today have little relation to Steiner's work, including circle time, math gnomes, or walls of rainbow hue. I believe, however, that, given our own limited insight, we must return again and again to Steiner's work to check our progress, our understanding, and our interpretation against what he said. Without this ongoing and recursive process—joyfully returning to the well from which our work springs—we risk implementing not creative, innovative, living teaching, but becoming an increasingly muddy copy of a copy of a copy. And there's little creative in that.

REFERENCES

Almon, J. (1999) Interview by Stephen Sagarin, tape recording, Toronto, June 25.

Association of Waldorf Schools of North America (AWSNA) (1999 and 2003) http://www.awsna.org.

Association of Waldorf Schools of North America (AWSNA). (2005) "Steps to Membership for Waldorf Schools." Second revision, June. http://www.awsna.org/pdf/StepsMembership6.14.pdf.

Association of Waldorf Schools of North America (AWSNA), including a partial listing of WECAN schools in U.S. (2011) http://www.members.awsna.org/Public/SchoolListPage.aspx.

Baravalle, H. (1963) *The International Waldorf School Movement*. Englewood, NJ: Waldorf School Monographs.

Barfield, O. (1966) *Romanticism Comes of Age*. Middletown, CT: Wesleyan University Press.

Barfield, O. (1971) *What Coleridge Thought*. Middletown, CT: Wesleyan University Press.

Barfield, O. (1979) *History, Guilt, and Habit*. Middletown, CT: Wesleyan University Press.

Barfield, O. (1988) *Saving the Appearances: A Study in Idolatry.* Middletown, CT: Wesleyan University Press.

Barnes, H. (1980) "An Introduction to Waldorf Education." In *Teachers College Record*, 81 (3), Spring 1980; pp. 322–336.

Barnes, H. (1998) Interview by Stephen Sagarin, tape recording, Ghent, NY, December 17.

Beard, C. (1913/1986) *An Economic Interpretation of the Constitution of the United States*. New York: The Free Press.

Bortoft, H. (1996) *The Wholeness of Nature: Goethe's Way Toward a Science of Conscious Participation in Nature.* Hudson, NY: Lindisfarne Press.

Brousseau, J. (1999) Interview by Stephen Sagarin, tape recording, Toronto, June 27.

Chafe, W. (1990) "America Since 1945." In *The New American History*, E. Foner, ed. Philadelphia: Temple U. Press.

Chase, A. (2000) "Harvard and the Making of the Unabomber." *Atlantic Monthly*, 285, 6, 41-65.

Coleridge, Samuel Taylor. *The Friend*. Barbara E. Rooke, ed. 2 Vols. Vol. 4 of the *Collected Works*. Princeton: Princeton University Press, (1969-present).

Cox, C. (2006) *In Search of Math Gnomes: First Grade Arithmetic in Waldorf Schools*. Unpublished M.S.Ed. thesis. Sunbridge College, NY.

Crain, W. (1992) *Theories of Development: Concepts and Applications*. Englewood Cliffs, NJ: Prentice-Hall.

Curran, P. (1990) Unpublished typescript.

Dugan, D. (1999) "Dan Dugan on his Sunbridge Experience." E-mail to: waldorf-critics@lists.best.com.

Dugan, D. (1999) http://www.dandugan.com/waldorf/index.html# Articles.

Easton, S. (1982) *Man and World in the Light of Anthroposophy*. Second, revised, edition. Spring Valley, NY: Anthroposophic Press.

Eddy, P. (1970) "The Waldorf School, Adelphi University." In *One Man's Vision: In Memoriam H.A.W. Myrin 1884-1970*. Proceedings, The Myrin Institute for Adult Education. New York, NY. Fall.

Edmunds, F. (1947) *Rudolf Steiner Education: The Waldorf Impulse*. London: Rudolf Steiner Press.

Elkind, D. (1981) *The Hurried Child: Growing Up Too Fast Too Soon*. Reading, MA: Addison-Wesley.

Emerson, R. (1966) "Education." In *Emerson On Education: Selections*, H. Jones, ed. New York: Teachers College Press.

Emerson, R. (2000) "History." In *The Essential Writings of Ralph Waldo Emerson*. B. Atkinson, ed. New York: Random House.

Emmet, B. (Undated) "From Farm to School: The Founding of the High Mowing School." Unpublished Typescript.

Emmet, B. (1991) Personal conversation, Wilton, New Hampshire, February 10.

Farber, D. (1994) "The Silent Majority and Talk about Revolution." In *The Sixties: From Memory to History*. D. Farber, ed. Chapel Hill: University of North Carolina Press.

Fox, M., ed. (1987) *Hildegard of Bingen's Book of Divine Works with Letters and Songs*. Santa Fe, NM: University of Santa Fe Press.

Fuchs, S. (2001) *Against Essentialism: A Theory of Culture and Society*. Cambridge, MA: Harvard.

Gardner, J. (1970) "The Founding of Adelphi's Waldorf School." In *One Man's Vision: In Memoriam, H.A.W. Myrin, 1884-1970*. Proceedings, The Myrin Institute for Adult Education, New York, NY. Fall 1970.

Gardner, J. (1975) *The Experience of Knowledge: Essays on American Education*. Garden City, NY: Waldorf Press.

Gardner, J. (1976) *Freedom for Education*. Washington, DC: Council for Educational Freedom.

Gardner, J. (1992) *Two Paths to the Spirit: Charismatic Christianity and Anthroposophy*. Great Barrington, MA: Golden Stone Press.

Gardner, J. (1996) *Education in Search of the Spirit: Essays on American Education*. (*The Experience of Knowledge: Essays on American Education*, 2nd ed.) Hudson, NY: Anthroposophic Press.

Gatto, J. (2002) *Dumbing Us Down*. Gabriola Island, BC, Canada: New Society Publishers.

Ginzburg, C. (1992) *The Cheese and the Worms: The Cosmos of a Sixteenth Century Miller*. J. and A. Tedeschi, trans. Baltimore, MD: The Johns Hopkins University Press.

Ginsburg, I. (1982) "Jean Piaget and Rudolf Steiner: Stages of Child Development and Implications for Pedagogy." *Teachers College Record*, 84 (2), pp. 327-337.

Gregg, E. (1970) "Kimberton Farms Agricultural School." In *One Man's Vision: In Memoriam, H.A.W. Myrin, 1884-1970*. Proceedings, The Myrin Institute for Adult Education, New York, NY. Fall 1970.

Gruber, H. *Darwin on Man: A Psychological Study of Scientific Creativity*. Chicago: University of Chicago Press, 1981.

Gruber, H. and Doris Wallace. *Creative People at Work*. New York: Oxford University Press, 1989.

Gruber, H. (1998) Personal conversation, New York, NY, April 14.

Habermas, J. (1987) *The Theory of Communicative Action, Vol. 2: Lifeworld and System: A Critique of Functionalist Reason*. T. McCarthy, trans. Boston: Beacon Press.

Hale, J. (1987) *The Education of a Yankee: An American Memoir.* New York: HarperCollins.

Harwood, A. (1958) *The Recovery of Man in Childhood: A Study in the Educational Work of Rudolf Steiner.* London: Hodder and Stoughton. (2001) Rev. 2nd ed. Great Barrington, MA: The Myrin Institute.

Heydebrand, C. (1966) *Curriculum of the First Waldorf School.* E. Hutchins, trans. London: Steiner Schools Fellowship.

Higham, J. (1962) "Beyond Consensus: The Historian as Moral Critic." *American Historical Review* 67, 609-25.

Hodgson, G. (1976) *American in Our Time.* Garden City, NY: Doubleday.

Hoffecker, G. (2010) Personal communication, telephone conversation, June 10.

Howard, S. (2006) "The Essentials of Waldorf Early Childhood Education." In *Gateways,* 51, Fall/Winter, pp. 6-12. Spring Valley, NY: Waldorf Early Childhood Association of North America.

James, H. (2008) *Hawthorne.* Tutis Digital Publishing.

Katz, M. (1989) *Reconstructing American Education.* Cambridge, MA: Harvard University Press.

Kelley, E. and M. Rasey. (1952) *Education and the Nature of Man.* New York: Harper & Brothers.

Lamb, G. (2004) *The Social Mission of Waldorf Education.* Ghent, NY: AWSNA Publications.

Lemisch, J. (1968) The American Revolution Seen From the Bottom Up. In *Towards a New Past: Dissenting Essays in American History,* Barton Bernstein, ed. New York: Knopf.

Lipson, M. (2002) Private communication, Great Barrington, MA, November 20.

Lovejoy, A. (1936 and 1964) *The Great Chain of Being: A Study of the History of an Idea.* Cambridge, MA: Harvard University Press.

Maynard, P. (2011) Personal communication, conversation, Great Barrington, MA, January 24.

McQuiston, J. (1979) "'Psychic' Ex-Student's Influence Shakes Waldorf School." *The New York Times.* Feb. 16.

Merleau-Ponty, M. (1964) *The Primacy of Perception and Other Essays on Phenomenological Psychology, the Philosophy of Art, History and Politics.* J. Edie, ed. Chicago: Northwestern University Press.

Morss, J. (1995) *Growing Critical: Alternatives to Developmental Psychology.* New York: Routledge.

Myrdal, G., et al. (1944/1996) *An American Dilemma: The Negro Problem and Modern Democracy.* Vol. 1. New York: Transaction Publishers.

Oberman, I. (1999) *Fidelity and Flexibility in Waldorf Education, 1919-1998.* Ann Arbor, MI: UMI Dissertation Services. UMI Number 9924473.

Oppenheimer, T. (1999) "Schooling the Imagination." *The Atlantic Monthly*, 284, 3, 71-83, September.

Papert, S. (1980) *Mindstorms: Children, Computers and Powerful Ideas.* New York: HarperCollins.

Piaget, J. (1935 and 1965) "Science of Education and the Psychology of the Child." In H. Gruber & J. Vonéche, eds. *The Essential Piaget.* Northvale, NJ: Jason Aronson.

Piaget, J. (1955) "The Stages of Intellectual Development in Childhood and Adolescence." In H. Gruber & J. Vonéche, eds. *The Essential Piaget.* Northvale, NJ: Jason Aronson.

Piaget, J. (1962) "The Role of Imitation in the Development of Representational Thought." In H. Gruber & J. Vonéche, eds. *The Essential Piaget.* Northvale, NJ: Jason Aronson.

Piaget, J. (1965) "Developments in Pedagogy." In H. Gruber & J. Vonéche, eds. *The Essential Piaget.* Northvale, NJ: Jason Aronson.

Piaget, J. (1966) "The Semiotic or Symbolic Function." In H. Gruber & J. Vonéche, eds. *The Essential Piaget.* Northvale, NJ: Jason Aronson.

Piaget, J. (1995) "Foreword." In H. Gruber & J. Vonéche, eds. *The Essential Piaget.* Northvale, NJ: Jason Aronson.

Piaget, J. and Inhelder, B. (1963) "Mental Images." In H. Gruber & J. Vonéche, eds. *The Essential Piaget.* Northvale, NJ: Jason Aronson.

Polanyi, M. (1983) *The Tacit Dimension.* Gloucester, MA: Peter Smith.

Portelli, A. (1991) *The Death of Luigi Trastulli and Other Stories: Form and Meaning in Oral History.* Albany, NY: State University of Albany Press.

Pratt, S. (1999) Telephone conversation, February 20.

Riccio, Mark-Dominick. (2002) *An Outline for a Renewal of Waldorf Education: Rudolf Steiner's Method of Heart-Thinking and Its Central Role in the Waldorf School.* Spring Valley, NY: Mercury Press.

Richards, M. C. (1980) *Toward Wholeness: Rudolf Steiner Education in America*. Middletown, CT: Wesleyan University Press.

Rose, G. (1996) Interview by Stephen Sagarin, tape recording, Garden City, NY, December 7.

Rudolf Steiner School Faculty and Board Meeting Minutes Archive, 1930-1950. New York, NY.

Sagarin, S. (2002) "No Such Thing: Recovering the Quality of Rudolf Steiner's Educational Work." In *Research Bulletin*, January 2003, Vol. VIII, No. 1. Hadley, MA: The Research Institute for Waldorf Education.

Sagarin, S. (2003) "Introduction: Recovering the Quality of Rudolf Steiner's Educational Work." In *What Is Waldorf Education?* Great Barrington, MA: SteinerBooks.

Sagarin, S. (2005) "The Seer and the Scientist: Rudolf Steiner and Jean Piaget on Children's Development." In *Research Bulletin*, December 2005, Vol. XI, No. 1, pp. 31-35. Wilton, NH: Research Institute for Waldorf Education.

Sagarin, S. (2007) "Playing 'Steiner Says:' Twenty Myths about Waldorf Education." In *Research Bulletin*, May 2007, Vol. XII, No. 2, pp. 37-44. Wilton, NH: Research Institute for Waldorf Education.

Sagarin, S. (2009) "What Makes Waldorf, Waldorf?" In Research Bulletin, Spring 2009, Vol. XIV, No. 1, pp. 25-32. Wilton, NH: Research Institute for Waldorf Education.

Sanders, G. (1999) Interview by Stephen Sagarin, tape recording, Toronto, June 25.

St. Charles, D. (1994) Interview by Alan Chartock on WAMC, 90.3 FM, Northeast Public Radio, Albany, NY. April; exact date unavailable. Reference obtained from undated cassette tape recording.

St. Charles, D. (2001) Interview by Stephen Sagarin, tape recording, Milwaukee, WI, February 21.

Schneider, L. (1999) Interview by Stephen Sagarin, tape recording, New York, NY, April 8.

Schwartz, E. (1999) *Millennial Child: Transforming Education in the Twenty-First Century*. Hudson, NY: Anthroposophic Press.

Shell, B. (1999) Interview by Stephen Sagarin, tape recording, Toronto, June 29.

Sloan, D. (1983) *Insight-Imagination: The Emancipation of Thought and the Modern World*. Westport, CT: Greenwood Publishing.

Sloan, D. (1996) "Reflections on the Evolution of Consciousness." In *Research Bulletin*, 1, 2 (June), 9-15. Spring Valley, NY: Waldorf Education Research Institute.

Sloan, D. (2004) "Declaration of Douglas Sloan in Support of Defendants' Opposition to Plaintiff's Motion for Summary Judgment…" Case No. CIV. S-98-0266 FCD PAN. PLANS, Inc. v. Sacramento City Unified School District, Twin Ridges Elementary School District, DOES 1-100. United States District Court, Eastern District of California. July 30, 2004.

Smilansky, S. and L. Shefatya. (1990) *Facilitating Play: A Medium for Promoting Cognitive, Socio-Emotional and Academic Development in Young Children*. Gaithersburg, MD: Psychosocial & Educational Publications.

Smith, P. (undated) "Taking a Risk in Education: Waldorf-Inspired Public Schools." Sunbridge College, NY.

Solzhenitsyn, A. (1978) *A World Split Apart: Commencement Address Delivered at Harvard University, June 8, 1978*. New York: Harper & Row.

Staley, B. (1998) "Introduction." In *Faculty Meetings With Rudolf Steiner*. Robert Lathe and Nancy Parsons Whittaker, trans. 2 volumes. Hudson, NY: Anthroposophic Press.

Staley, B. (1999) Interview by Stephen Sagarin, tape recording, Great Barrington, MA, March 5 and 17.

Steiner, R. (1965) *The Education of the Child in the Light of Anthroposophy* (from GA 34). 2nd English ed. G. & M. Adams, trans. New York: Anthroposophic Press. See "The Education of the Child in the Light of Spiritual Science" (from GA 34) in *The Education of the Child and Early Lectures on Education* (1996). Foundations of Waldorf Education series. Great Barrington, MA: Anthroposophic Press.

Steiner, R. (1967) *Discussions With Teachers*. Helen Fox, trans. London: Rudolf Steiner Press.

Steiner, R. (1970) *The Philosophy of Freedom*. 7th English edition. Michael Wilson, trans. London: Rudolf Steiner Press.

Steiner, R. (1972) *Curative Education*. GA 317. M. Adams, trans. London: Rudolf Steiner Press.

Steiner, R. (1990a) *The Christmas Conference for the Foundation of the General Anthroposophical Society 1923/1924.* J. Collis, trans. Hudson, NY: Anthroposophic Press.

Steiner, R. (1990b) *The Universal Human: The Evolution of Individuality.* Four lectures given between 1909 and 1916 in Munich and Bern. Bamford, C. and S. Seiler, trans. Anthroposophic Press: [no city]. See especially pp. 12–13.

Steiner, R. (1992) *Towards Social Renewal: Basic Issues of the Social Question.* Bristol, UK: Rudolf Steiner Press.

Steiner, R. (1994) *Theosophy: An Introduction to the Spiritual Processes in Human Life and in the Cosmos.* Hudson, NY: Anthroposophic Press.

Steiner, R. (1995) *Intuitive Thinking as a Spiritual Path: A Philosophy of Freedom.* M. Lipson, trans. Great Barrington, MA: Anthroposophic Press.

Steiner, R. (1995a) "A Lecture for Prospective Parents. August 31, 1919." *In The Spirit of the Waldorf School: Lectures Surrounding the Founding of the First Waldorf School*, Stuttgart, 1919. R. Lathe and N. Whittaker, trans. Anthroposophic Press: Hudson, NY.

Steiner, R. (1995b) "The Fundamentals of Waldorf Education." November 11, 1921. In *Waldorf Education and Anthroposophy 1: Nine Public Lectures.* Anthroposophic Press: Hudson, NY.

Steiner, R. (1996a) *The Education of the Child* [from GA 34] *and Early Lectures on Education.* Great Barrington, MA: SteinerBooks.

Steiner, R. (1996b) *Foundations of Human Experience.* Robert Lathe and Nancy Parsons Whittaker, trans. CW 293. Hudson, NY: Anthroposophic Press, 1996.

Steiner, R. (1997) *The Roots of Education.* 5 Lectures, Berne, 1924. CW 309. Great Barrington, MA: SteinerBooks. 1997.

Steiner, R. (2000) *Practical Advice to Teachers.* 14 Lectures, Stuttgart, 1919. CW 294. Great Barrington, MA: SteinerBooks.

Steiner, R. (2003) *Soul Economy: Body, Soul, and Spirit in Waldorf Education.* 16 Lectures, Dornach, 1921-1922. CW 303. Great Barrington, MA: SteinerBooks. 2003.

Stockmeyer, E.A.K. (1969/1985) *Rudolf Steiner's Curriculum for Waldorf Schools.* R. Everett–Zade, trans. Forest Row, E. Sussex, U.K.: Steiner Schools Fellowship.

Talbott, S. (1995) *The Future Does Not Compute: Transcending the Machines In Our Midst*. Sebastopol, CA: O'Reilly and Associates.

Taylor-Weaver, U. (undated) "Faculty Meetings—College of Teachers." http://www.bobnancy.com/bobnancy.html.

Tomlinson, A. (1999) Interview by Stephen Sagarin, tape recording, Hempstead, NY, April 9.

Traub, J. (2000) "Schools Are Not the Answer." *New York Times Magazine*, January 16.

Waldorf Early Childhood Association of North America (2002). "Waldorf Early Childhood Programs and Initiatives." Spring Valley, NY.

Waldorf Early Childhood Association of North America (WECAN) schools in U.S. (2011) http://www.waldorfearlychildhood.org/membership_directory.asp.

Wannamaker, O. (1928) "Rudolf Steiner: An Introduction to His Life and Thought." In *Rudolf Steiner School Quarterly*, January–April 1928: Rudolf Steiner Educational Union, New York.

Whitehead, A. (1929/1967) *The Aims of Education and Other Essays*. New York: Free Press.

Whittaker, N. (2001) Post to subscribers of the list server Waldorf@ maelstrom.stjohns.edu. Feb. 11. Subscribe at http://www.bobnancy.com. Quoted with author's permission.

Wieneke, H. (1970) "Mr. Myrin." In *One Man's Vision: In Memoriam, H.A.W. Myrin, 1884-1970*. Proceedings, The Myrin Institute for Adult Education: New York, NY. Fall.

Williams, L. (1997) "The Oak Meadow Trilogy." Oak Meadow, Inc. http://www.oakmeadow.com/resources/articles/Trilogy.htm.

Wilmes, L. and Dick Wilmes. (1983) *Everyday Circle Times*. No city of publication specified: Building Blocks.

Wilson, F. (1998) *The Hand: How Its Use Shapes the Brain, Language, and Human Culture*. New York: Vintage Books.

Winkler, F. (1970) "Recollections of Alarik W. Myrin." In *One Man's Vision: In Memoriam, H.A.W. Myrin, 1884-1970*. Proceedings, The Myrin Institute for Adult Education: New York, NY.

Winnicott, D. W. (1996) *Thinking about Children*. Eds. Ray Shepherd, Jennifer Johns, and Helen Taylor Robinson. New York: Addison-Wesley Publishing Co., Inc.

Winter, D. (1999) Interview by Stephen Sagarin, tape recording, Toronto, June 26.

Winter, D. (1999) "America's Gold Rush: Can It Be Redeemed?" Talks given June 25 and 26, 1999, Toronto, Canada, AWSNA conference.

ACKNOWLEDGMENTS

This work is based in large part on my Ph.D. dissertation, *Promise and Compromise: A History of Waldorf Schools in the United States, 1928-1998*. As such, particular thanks are due to the guidance, insight, and support of my sponsor, Douglas Sloan; the care, subtlety and humor of my second reader, Robert McCaughey; and the rest of my dissertation committee: Professors Hope Leichter, Thomas Sobol, and Callie Waite.

Other professors to whom I am grateful include developmental psychologists Howard Gruber and John Broughton; philosopher Helmut Peukert, who imparted his clarity and his understanding of the work of, especially, Dewey and Habermas; historian David Armitage, who introduced me to the work of Carlo Ginzburg; and historian Ronald Grele, who introduced me to the field of oral history.

Thanks especially to those who sat for interviews, without which this would be a less lively and life-like history: Allegra Allesandri, Joan Almon, Henry Barnes, John Brousseau, Cheryl Colbert, Beulah Emmet, Douglas Gerwin, George Hoffecker, Betty Krainis, Patrice Maynard, Robert Norris, Susan Olsen, Swain Pratt, Chip Romer, George Rose, Dorothy St. Charles, Grace Sanders, Lucy Schneider, Eugene Schwartz, Barbara Shell, Betty Staley, Al Tomlinson, and Dorit Winter.

Thanks also to those who helped to guide me through this maze, in ways large and small but all equally deserving of gratitude: David Alsop, Susan Braun, Martha Collins, Lisa Daniels, David Dozier, Anne Eaton, Winslow Eliot, Renni Greenberg Gallagher, Mark and Adrian Gardner, Antje Ghaznavi, Pamela Giles, Peter Goble, Susan and Michael Howard, Kathryn Humphrey, David and Christine Inglis, Cher Levendosky, Michael Lipson and Holly Morse, Bob and Sarah Mayer, Joe Proskauer, Roland Rothenbucher, George and Leonore Russell, Robert Schiappacasse, Ernst Schubert, Virginia Sease, David Sloan, Patrick Smalley, Patti Smith, Bruce Travins, Uta Taylor-Weaver, and Christopher Young. Some of these know me well and some may barely remember me, but I took notes when they spoke.

Thanks to my students, all of them. Yes, all of them.

Thanks to my colleagues at Sunbridge Institute; in particular, Cat Greenstreet, Jana Hawley, George McWilliam, and Stefan Vdoviak.

Thanks to a travel grant from the Future Values Fund of the Rudolf Steiner Foundation that made possible portions of the chapter, "The Alternatives."

Thanks to Stephen Hadrovic and Walter Stuber who, independently, virtually ordered me to pursue my degree—and therefore the research on which this book is based—and who kicked me when I balked.

Thanks to Jeffrey Kane and James Madsen, who talked me through the first inklings of my topic.

Thanks to Donna Chirico, Cair Crawford, Janet Gerson, Mary Lee Grisanti, and Howie Schaffer, the best of graduate school friends.

Thanks (again) to Douglas Gerwin and to David Mitchell for their support at the Research Institute for Waldorf Education.

Thanks to the Rudolf Steiner Library in Ghent, New York, and the librarians who put up with my years of overdue books: Judith Keily, Jude Neu-Limburger, Fred Paddock, and Judith Soleil.

Thanks to the Rudolf Steiner School, New York City, for access to faculty meeting minutes.

Thanks to the Rudolf Steiner Foundation Future Values Fund for a travel grant that made possible visits to Milwaukee, Wisconsin, and the Pine Ridge Reservation, South Dakota.

Thanks to my patient and encouraging wife, Janis Martinson; my children, Andrew and Kathleen; my mother, Sally Young; and my father, David.

And thanks to my editors, Christopher Bamford and Colleen Shetland, and the support of Gene Gollogly, of SteinerBooks, without whose interest, insight, patience, and prodding this book would not exist.

The work of all makes possible the work of one. Shortfalls, of course, are mine alone.